*FROM HEAVEN TO EARTH:*

# SCHWEITZER RETURNS

BY ROBERT R. LEICHTMAN, M.D.

*The Thirteenth In A Series*

**ARIEL PRESS**
THE PUBLISHING HOUSE OF LIGHT
COLUMBUS, OHIO

*Second Printing*

This book is made possible by gifts
to the Publications Fund of Light.

SCHWEITZER RETURNS
*Copyright © 1980 by Light*

*All Rights Reserved. No part of this book may be used or reproduced in any manner whatsoever without written permission, except in the case of brief quotations embodied in articles and reviews. Printed in the United States of America. Direct all inquiries to Ariel Press, P.O. Box 20580, Columbus, Ohio 43220.*

ISBN 0-89804-063-9

## ALBERT SCHWEITZER RETURNS:

"The evidence of the beauty and joy of life is always present, even in the physical world, as imperfect as it is. Even in the jungle we could find it. Even in darkest Africa we could find evidence of God's light and love and beauty. It's in the people, it's in the country. It's not that difficult to find."

"Socialism is antispiritual by nature, whether or not religion is banned, because it dehumanizes the individual. It dehumanizes society. All of life becomes a bureaucracy in a socialist country."

"Spiritual healing is a natural companion to the scientific techniques used by the average physician in his daily practice. It doesn't replace them, but neither should medicine replace the spiritual side of healing. They ought to complement each other."

"When I was playing Bach, I found God in the midst of the music. It was a very real, joyous experience for me. I found God's love and peace and order and wholeness while playing Bach. I became consumed in my spirit."

"If you are a person who expects to attain instant enlightenment, you are probably also a person who will stop after making very little progress, and just stay there, believing that you've accomplished what you set out to do. You've gained your instant's worth, and so you stop."

—Albert Schweitzer

# PRIESTS OF GOD

From the beginning of civilization, men and women have lifted their eyes above the chores, travails, and delights of earth and sought to communicate with heaven. Some have looked toward heaven as the abode of those who have departed; missing their loved ones, they have wanted reassurance that they continued to survive. Others, regarding heaven as the kingdom of God, have sought to contact it so that they might worship God and His creation more completely. Still others have thought of heaven as a perfected ideal to be honored, aspired to, and invoked in time of crisis and need. For some, heaven represented the source of all creativity, wisdom, and genius; inspired and led by its light, they have sought to serve that light as effectively as possible.

We are entering a new era, and as we do, new opportunities to communicate with heaven, and bring heaven to earth, are arising. It is no longer necessary to regard heaven as a faraway place somewhere ''up there,'' unapproachable to all save a few select mediums, prophets, philosophers, or geniuses. Every human being, sincere of purpose and loving in nature, has the capacity to rise above the mundane and find heaven, be inspired by it, and enrich his or her life with its beauty and joy.

Yet many people do not recognize the opportunity before them. Some, of course, have little knowledge of the nature of heaven and its accessibility. But others are knowledgeable enough; they have worshipped heaven, prayed to it, read about it, and hope to arrive there someday themselves. But they are too much in awe of the whole idea of heaven to think in terms of bringing it to earth in their own lives, *now*.

It was in order to demonstrate the closeness and relevance of heaven to our own lives that I undertook the first series of twelve interviews, From Heaven to Earth, which has already been published. In those twelve books, I chose to interview the spirits of many of the outstanding psychics and mediums of the last one hundred years—people such as Edgar Cayce, C.W. Leadbeater, Stewart Edward White, and H.P. Blavatsky—for they performed a remarkable service in demonstrating the basic principles of communicating with heaven, not just the heaven of human afterlife, but even more importantly, the heaven of our inner wisdom. *That*, after all, is the kingdom of God, the home of the perfected ideal, and the source of the creativity of genius. I also chatted with the spirits of several outstanding individuals not directly involved in the psychic world, but nonetheless inspired—people such as Carl Jung, William Shakespeare, Thomas Jefferson, and Nikola Tesla—to encourage readers to broaden their understanding of the nature and scope of heaven.

These initial interviews illustrated that the world of spirits is always around us—and is available, from time to time, to help us meet our creative needs. The spirits are not interested in doing our work for us, but do respond to the invitation to cooperate with physical people. The first series also set forth the idea that genius and creativity are inspired activities—inspired not so much by spirits, but from the "kingdom of heaven" within us. With the spirits, I explored the nature of genius—its development and expression, and how to focus it on earth. To me, one of the most significant points made by the first series is that it is not only man's *heritage*, but also his *obligation* to tap the inner divine wisdom available to him.

I have been gratified by the response to these interviews. Many readers have commented to me how reading these books has spurred them on to new realizations of their own inner life. And many have also encouraged me to follow up the first set of twelve interviews with yet another. Some have even suggested the names of spirits they would like to see interviewed!

The spirits themselves wasted little time indicating that they, too, were interested in a second series. But I knew another set could not just be "more of the same." To be worthwhile, every project has to grow as it unfolds. It has to reach out and touch something new. A project cannot just rest on its reputation, or it dies.

And so, for quite awhile, I did not even bother trying to decide whom to contact in a second series. Instead, I thought it was more important to decide *why*

I ought to contact them! I am not one to embark on an activity just because it is appealing, or sounds like fun, or because others expect it of me. I want to be sure the work will be a valuable contribution and bear fruit.

In pondering the purpose of a second series, I am sure I was guided to a great extent by the spirits who have supervised this project from the beginning. Gradually, the intent began to take form in my mind, as follows.

The ultimate reason why we strive to contact the kingdom of heaven is to become an agent of God's light, illuminating the darkness wherever it exists and spiritualizing civilization and the earth through all that we do. It is not enough to be a devotee of an abstract God, Who sits on a throne somewhere apart from humanity. Nor is it sufficient to sing hymns of praise and confess our sins. The enlightened person does more; he worships God by serving His evolutionary plans. He becomes a steward of life here on earth, and by example, leads others to do the same. Frequently, he is not even perceived by the masses as a servant or worshipper of God, because his field of endeavor is not within the traditional scope of religion; yet he knows heaven, loves God, and serves the Plan.

Such a person could truly be called a *priest of God*, not in the conventional sense of a somber ecclesiastic garbed in black, but as an agent of light who practices the presence of God in everything he does. Eventually, we are all meant to become priests of God in this sense, and should strive toward that goal. Although this destiny is still a future one for most of us, nonetheless there have always been true priests of God with us, serving heaven, leading humanity, and healing the imperfections of earth. Indeed, many of the greatest servants of God mankind has ever known have walked this earth, touching heaven, within the last three centuries.

As this thought occurred to me, I knew I had found the purpose of the second set of interviews—to demonstrate how contemporary priests of God have revealed divine wisdom, love, and talent as they worked to enrich civilization and culture in all its many facets—in government, the arts, literature, music, science, medicine, industry, philosophy, religion, and education.

Armed with this thought, I began to consider the qualifications I should look for in choosing the spirits to interview. To my mind, the priest of God is a person who is able to find God in the midst of everyday life and, by the power, inspiration, and refinement of his talent and understanding, manifest something divine in his work. He brings heaven to earth—not just to worship it and reveal it, *but to use it to transform the world!* He does not necessarily conduct services in churches or temples, but renders service where it is needed, to teach and enlighten, to beautify, to lead in times of crisis, to help harness physical resources for human use, and to heal both individuals and society.

Having outlined these criteria in my mind, the choices emerged quite rapidly. I immediately thought of the Dutch artist Rembrandt van Rijn, who was surely a priest of the paintbrush. In music, many choices could have been made, but the composer Richard Wagner stood out clearly as a high priest of spiritual purpose. Who is not swept into a vision of heaven in listening to his operas?

I chose Mark Twain in literature. As priests of leadership, I selected Sir Winston Churchill, who led not just England but all of civilized humanity through the crisis of World War II, and Abraham Lincoln, who healed a badly divided nation with charity and patience. Benjamin Franklin could certainly be thought of as a priest of leadership, too, but I believe it even more appropriate to recognize him for his contributions to diplomacy and philosophy.

Albert Einstein was an easy choice as a priest of science, a man who used his mind as his primary scientific instrument. Also from the world of science, I selected Luther Burbank, the horticultural wizard. In industry, I thought of Andrew Carnegie, who built a fortune in steel and then set a model for enlightened philanthropy, using his wealth to fund public libraries throughout the nation and support other worthwhile charities and public projects.

I also wanted to interview representative priests of enlightened service. In this category, I chose Dr. Albert Schweitzer, whose hospital in Africa became a symbol of unselfish Christian service, and Paramahansa Yogananda, the Hindu mystic who brought many of the spiritual teachings of India to America and helped inspire new interest in this country in the life of spirit.

Each of these great individuals richly deserves the title ''priest of God.'' Not only did they work with brilliance and genius in their chosen fields, which is significant enough, but they also were healers of society. Only Dr. Schweitzer treated broken physical bodies, but all of them healed, to some extent, the broken aspirations, the diseases, and the confusion of humanity as a whole. Churchill healed by stopping the aggression of fascism. Mark Twain healed with his pen; his literary masterpieces, so often regarded today as stories for youth, actually served to enlighten the American public to a new sensitivity regarding racial discrimination and the value of human individuality. Wagner and Rembrandt healed ugliness. Carnegie worked to heal, by example and by contribution, the intense materialism of the past century. Burbank, Einstein, and Yogananda healed ignorance. Franklin and Lincoln were two of the prime contributors to the health of America as a nation.

All qualify as priests of God in another way, too—through their work, they brought a fresh revelation of God's light and love to meet our modern needs. They did not just recycle old approaches to living; they *innovated*, in profound and spiritual ways. Einstein's new ideas in physics have stretched the minds of many an individual who has sought to comprehend them. Yogananda and Schweitzer touched thousands of people with a higher quality of God's love than they had ever encountered before. Lincoln and Franklin lifted the concepts of community and brotherhood to new levels of nobility.

As I began conducting the interviews, I came to appreciate how appropriate the concept of ''priests of God'' actually is. Although all of these individuals are well-known to history, I discovered that we really know very little about their true humanity and scope of character. History all too often traps itself in the mundane details of the lives of great people, striving for ''objectivity'' but forgetting that the subjective elements of genius are even more interesting. As a result, we tend to miss the fact that some people go far beyond the common motives and activities of ordinary people, and strive to reach a higher level of achievement. I was delighted to find, however, that all the spirits I had tapped were quite eager to talk about the spiritual impulses which drove them in their work—indeed, sometimes drove them to sacrifice their well-being, their fortunes, and their health. They also talked candidly about the inspiration which guided them, the dedication and love that kept them going, and their views on the dignity and nobility of mankind. That, after all, is what is truly important about each of these gentlemen—not the details of their work and lives.

The spirits also took an obvious interest in the whole development of the series itself. This is perhaps best attested to by the fact that, part way through the process of arranging and conducting the interviews, several of them suggested that the twelfth and final book in this second series ought to depart from the usual format. I asked them what they suggested. In reply, they recommended a ''round-table'' discussion of the destiny and the future of America, involving a number of spirits, all of whom have been prominent in influencing the history of this country. Some would be founding fathers; others would be from more recent periods of American history. Some might have already appeared in earlier interviews; others would be fresh voices. The object would be to reveal more fully than ever before the nature of the Spirit of America—and the responsibility of each citizen to help fulfill its destiny.

That, then, will be the twelfth and final book—*The Destiny of America*. To me, it will be a demonstration of how a whole nation has the opportunity to become a "priest of God," if the citizens so choose.

In introducing this second series of interviews to the public, it would perhaps be useful to restate certain basic tenets. First, I did not conduct these interviews in order to prove, either to myself or to anyone else, the fact of survival after death. I have accepted this basic fact of life for many, many years, based on my own experiences. It is as natural for me to contact heaven and converse with spirits as it is to breathe or eat or sleep. It is a daily occurrence.

Nor would it serve any purpose to write another book to prove the issue of survival—or to demonstrate that it is possible to communicate with "spooks," as I affectionately call my friends in spirit. Dozens of carefully documented and well-written books have been authored during the past century for the express purpose of proving these points; I have little interest in "reinventing the wheel." For those who still question the reality of survival after death, or mediumistic communication, I would recommend reading these other books. A recent paperback by John G. Fuller on the work of Eileen Garrett and others, called *The Airmen Who Would Not Die*, is an excellent place to begin. So is *Our Unseen Guest*, by Darby and Joan; *The Betty Book*, by Stewart Edward White; and the writings of Sir Oliver Lodge.

Second, in reading the interviews in *From Heaven to Earth*, it is a good idea to keep in mind that these people have not remained frozen in time since they "died." Spirits do change and continue to evolve after they leave behind the physical body. Indeed, the personality of an individual may undergo so many evolutionary changes as a spook that it virtually disappears in time, until all that survives is the innermost spirit—the real essence of our human life. The evolution of consciousness, after all, is an inherent fact of life. It is often delayed, and even obstructed, by some personalities, but in other individuals it can occur quite rapidly, once the physical body has been discarded. This has been very much the case for many of the people I interviewed, both in the first and second series. It is for this reason that several of them have declared views of life which differ greatly from opinions they held while on earth. They have simply outgrown the more limited perspectives they once held!

In the first series, for example, Sigmund Freud announced that he is no longer a Freudian in the way he views human nature and its treatment in psychotherapy. In the new series, Luther Burbank talks at some length about the cooperation he had from the angelic kingdom in performing his work—something he was not consciously aware of while in the physical. Certainly, neither we nor the spirits themselves lose anything valuable as a result of these changes. Instead, it gives us a better opportunity to appreciate the *essence* of their individuality and genius—the spiritualized aspect of what was once their earthly personality. It is this fragment of "spirit" that I conversed with.

That concept may take some getting used to, to put it in popular parlance, but to me it is an idea with wonderful potentiality. Because spirits evolve, it becomes possible for them to do things which were impossible for them while on earth. Einstein, for instance, states that he is able to follow the evolution of matter as it roams the solar system and moves from one plane to another, from the most sublime to the very densest aspects of earth, as we know it with our physical senses.

While many spirits lack the imagination and ambition to make these changes—just as they failed to evolve and grow very much while in physical form—men and women of genius are still fired by their zest to comprehend life and its phenomena as much as possible. Therefore, the interviews are lively, informative, and always thought-provoking.

If mediumship is ever to reach its fullest potential—which is enormous—the evolution and growth of spirits must be taken into account, and honored. Too often, mediumship and clairaudient communication with spirits are practiced at very low levels—to obtain simple messages and reassurances from departed friends and relatives. Even when they are taken to a somewhat higher level, they still tend to be imprisoned by superstition and preconceptions of what the heaven worlds are like. "Spirit guides," for example, are invariably treated as exalted beings to be worshipped and followed without question. This silly attitude demeans the whole value and practice of mediumship—and is a dangerous departure into fantasy.

The enlightened use of mediumship should be to bring to earth ideas, insights, and energies which can enrich our lives and help us become better people. That is not possible, of course, unless we can have an *intelligent* conversation with an *intelligent* spirit through an *intelligent* medium. That is a goal worth aspiring to—but hardly the norm in the general practice of mediumship.

Fortunately, effective mediumship is not limited to the practice of falling into a deep trance in a dimly lit room. Any person who seeks to prepare his or her mind and then avidly searches for insight into the phenomena of life can make contact with the realm of spirit. That may not involve going into trance or seeing clairvoyant visions at all; the spirits may just be "felt" as intelligent presences. But the insight and ideas do come, and are valuable.

My aim in presenting these interviews is not to encourage readers to rush out to the nearest medium and have a conversation with departed friends. Nor is it to convince skeptics. My intent is to present valuable ideas and to stimulate deeper reflection about the purposes and nature of human life. Each reader must decide for himself or herself the value of the ideas set forth in these books; they are neither cast in bronze nor meant to be canonized. Instead, I hope each reader will test the ideas with his or her own common sense, pondering on possible ways to apply them and exploring their implications.

It may, of course, be legitimately asked how I know that I was indeed communicating with the spirits I claim to have interviewed. How do I know that I was speaking with the spirit of Mark Twain and not just the subconscious of the medium—or even a different spirit who was masquerading as Twain? What proof or evidence do I have to support the identity of these communicators?

The only proof I offer is the substance of the interviews themselves. From long experience, I have learned that there is no "evidence" which cannot be faked by clever but devious mediums—or, even worse, clever but devious spooks. Certainly, mannerisms are easily imitated and prove nothing. But most of the evidence which investigators of spiritualistic phenomena covet so greatly is not really substantial proof of "spirit," either. It is evidence only of the remnants of personality. The life of spirit is something far, far greater—and it is time we stopped degrading our vision of heaven with what are essentially materialistic demands and beliefs.

I was impressed that Albert Schweitzer was the person he claimed to be because he spoke and acted like a person who had a great reverence for life. He demonstrated profound insight into the higher qualities of human and divine nature. No spirit or medium who actually possessed insight of that caliber would gain anything by posing as Schweitzer; indeed, he would have outgrown the temptation to deceive and mislead long, long ago. Therefore, it is reasonable to accept that interview at face value.

Just so, I accepted Rembrandt because he spoke like an artistic genius; I welcomed Einstein because the brilliance of his comments could have come from only one source: Einstein himself.

Naturally, I had other reasons to be reasonably confident that the spirits I interviewed were the people I had actually summoned. For one thing, I have been assisted in this project from the very beginning by a small group of spirits whom I know to be of the highest integrity and quality. I have a long and intimate acquaintance with these spirits; they are quite expert at detecting "ringers." Their endorsement of the identity of each of these individuals is a very high recommendation.

But the most impressive evidence, to me, is the power and presence of the spirits themselves. When Schweitzer appeared, for instance, the whole room was flooded with an intensely strong quality of devotion and reverence, which affected everyone listening. It stayed until he left. When Churchill spoke, I sensed the magnetic power of a true leader. In the interview with Benjamin Franklin, I had a devil of a time getting him to comment on specific aspects of current American policy. Even in heaven, apparently, he is very much the diplomat, carefully choosing his words and weighing their impact.

To some, these "proofs" may seem suspiciously subjective—but then, our contact with the realm of spirit is entirely subjective in nature. It is not possible to verify psychic and mediumistic realities with machines or statistics. It is only possible to verify them by evaluating the significance of the ideas and guidance produced. Any reader who finds that disappointing is in need of redefining his understanding of spirit.

The spirits join me in submitting these ideas and insights for careful inspection and evaluation. They do not really care whether or not they are believed to be real—as long as their ideas are considered objectively and with an open mind. They certainly do not want anyone to accept these ideas in the belief that they passed through hallowed lips. Nor do they wish to be worshipped.

The ultimate value of these interviews, in fact, lies not in the identity of those participating—or even in the substance of the ideas. It lies in the capacity of each reader to comprehend and use these ideas, and thereby bring heaven to earth in his or her life.

In that endeavor, the spirits and I wish you all the best of luck.

—Robert R. Leichtman, M.D.

# ALBERT SCHWEITZER RETURNS

Perhaps the best way to describe the life and work of Albert Schweitzer is to liken it to a finely cut diamond, sparkling in brilliant sunlight. Schweitzer was a man of multiple facets—not a jack of all trades, but a genius of the highest order. His greatest and most enduring fame, of course, comes from his work as a medical missionary in equatorial Africa. There, he built and equipped a hospital from his own income, and devoted the final fifty years of his life to treating the medical needs of the natives. But it is also important to realize that Albert Schweitzer was *already* a famous individual before he decided to become a doctor and go to Africa. He held a university chair in theology, and his book, *The Quest for the Historical Jesus*, had established him as a world figure in his field. He was also recognized as one of the leading interpreters of his time of the music of Johann Sebastian Bach, and was in popular demand for organ concerts.

To renounce such recognition and pursue an entirely

new career—and in a God-forbidding place such as the African jungle of 1915—surely must have struck Schweitzer's contemporaries as sheer madness. But diamonds are of special merit; they are of a higher quality than emeralds or pearls or other precious gems. So was Schweitzer. It is not credible to believe that *his* genius and love were just another accident in time and space. His lifetime and accomplishments are obviously the consequence of enormous talent, dedication, wisdom, and hard work. He was, indeed, *more* than a diamond—he was a diamond sparkling in brilliant sunlight. He was a man who revealed, through all that he did, the powerful presence of God within him.

The renunciation of comfort, position, and fame was actually a very logical step for Schweitzer to take. While other theologians were content to preach and discuss religious concepts, Schweitzer firmly believed that religion should be honored in one's daily activities and duties. Unless charity, love, faith, and goodwill are brought to life in a meaningful way in our own self-expression, they are dead—for us. And yet, as Schweitzer observed, these qualities of consciousness are far too frequently left unexpressed.

In his day as well as our own, for example, the concept of charity was often reduced to the intimidation and manipulation of people to donate money, time, and effort as a means of expiating guilty feelings about the imperfections of the world. Charitable work was often left to the direction of people who were more puffed up with righteousness or smugness, than motivated by a genuine sense of love and caring. Moreover, far too many people involved in service plodded through their work with boredom, resentment, and a confused sense of duty, rather than cheerfulness and a willingness to help.

In his service in Africa, however, Dr. Schweitzer set an example of caring and dedication which richly deserves to be considered the work of a priest of God. In his patient, gentle way, he demonstrated what genuine love is, and the purpose it serves. For him, love was not just another four-letter word to be used in lectures and sermons to intimidate others into being more guilty or contrite. It was a powerful force within himself—and within every human being—which helped him view all of life as a noble creation of a loving God. Love helped him be aware of the magnificence of God, and His presence in all things; it drew him into communion with the creative and healing potential in all life forms. Love motivated him to act with kindness and wisdom, and to be an agent of its benevolence and greatness in all that he did. Love gave him the vision to see the needs of people, and supported him as he sought to relieve their distress. Love lifted him up so he could comprehend the inner dimension of life; it enabled him to endure in spite of the misery he confronted every day. Love revealed to him the beauty in all things—and led him to enter into oneness with God's great love for His entire creation.

It should be little wonder, then, that Dr. Schweitzer turned to a desolate and forgotten area of the planet to initiate his medical mission. Where else was there a greater need for intelligent and compassionate service? Where else was there a less civilized, more harsh country in which to work? Where else was there a greater opportunity to demonstrate the healing and transforming power of divine love?

The obstacles he had to overcome to perform this service were formidable. When he and his wife Hélenè arrived in Lambaréné, in what is now the African nation of Gabon, they did not step into someone else's shoes. They had to build a hospital with their own hands, teach the natives the value of medical care, overcome the superstitions and fears of the local tribes, and work, at least in the beginning, with very little support.

During World War I, Schweitzer was sent to France as a prisoner of war—because he happened to be born German. That interrupted his missionary service, but gave him a chance to write. After the war, however, he returned to Lambaréné and reconstructed the hospital. At the time of his death in 1965, the hospital had grown to the point of being able to care for 350 patients, plus their relatives. A nearby leper colony Schweitzer had also founded cared for 150 patients.

For this work "on behalf of the Brotherhood of Nations," and his writings, Dr. Schweitzer was awarded the Nobel Peace Prize in 1952.

To my mind, Schweitzer's work in Africa illustrates three important features of genuine service. First, it must be motivated by a sincere love and regard for all of life—what he called "the reverence for life." We do not serve only those whom we like and those who will like us in return, or repay us. We serve where there is a need. Second, an individual who would serve should have the capacity to serve cheerfully, without a martyr complex and without selfish motives for doing so. The service should be seen as a way of honoring the life of the spirit, not as a terrible duty to be performed to a chorus of moaning and groaning.

And third, we must not treat the people we serve with condescension or "holier than thou" smugness. Dr. Schweitzer served because he cared about the welfare of the people he sought to help. He saw them as children of God with needs to be met—not as savage natives or stupid heathens to be converted.

In this regard, it seems to me that Dr. Schweitzer's service was not limited to the tiny compound of Lambaréné. The direct beneficiaries of his loving care were the African citizens of Gabon, but indirectly, the whole of Western civilization profited. Dr. Schweitzer returned to Europe numerous times, giving concert and lecture tours to raise money for his mission. As he did, he helped educate thousands of Westerners to look beyond their personal needs and help support the work of Christian charity wherever it might be focused.

I am also deeply impressed by what Dr. Schweitzer gave up in order to perform this service. He could have made much more money, directly touched the lives of more people, and enjoyed himself far more if he had pursued his musical gifts as a full-time career. His expertise and interest in music were such that he became a world authority on the reconstruction of ancient organs—even while working in Africa! Certainly it would have been an easy rationalization to make, especially after being taken prisoner of war, to abandon the hospital in Africa and pursue more comfortable activities. But he did not. He returned again and again to Africa and worked to add to his hospital and staff. Even as an aged man, he continued to render excellent health care to the people of Lambaréné.

I doubt that the temptation to abandon his work

ever entered Dr. Schweitzer's mind, however. The type of service he performed, honestly motivated by spiritual love, tends to be an activity which is pursued without doubts, rationalizations, or hesitations. The personality that is dominated by the love of the innermost spirit automatically acts as an agent of goodwill to do those things which serve the one life. In this regard, the service of an enlightened individual is just as natural as the reflexive blinking of our eyes when we are surprised by a loud noise.

Those who knew Dr. Schweitzer well often tell of his quiet and thoughtful patience and gentleness. As tired as he might be, for example, he would still sit down to answer his mail, knowing how important the letters could be to those receiving them. As exhausted as he might be, he always had time for visitors as well as patients.

In the interview that follows, Dr. Schweitzer talks extensively about what was obviously one of his favorite themes—the nature of loving service. He comments on his idea of resignation or renunciation, removing it from the usual context of self-annihilation and placing it in the more dignified, enlightened perspective of discovering the inner life of spirit, our individual connection with God. Repeatedly, he encourages us to make the effort to establish these inner links with spirit.

I also inquired about his philosophy of ''reverence for life,'' which he wrote about extensively in his later books, especially his *Philosophy of Civilization* and *Out of My Life and Thought*. He comments that love alone is not enough to guarantee effective service; it must be activated by the will to do good works. As he puts it, it must become the *will to love* and the *will to life*.

In answer to questions, Dr. Schweitzer also comments on perceptions he made in his writings regarding the problems of pessimism and skepticism in world thought, as well as the nature of evil. This highly thoughtful man has some very strong convictions about these subjects—and about the responsibility of each human being to learn to think for himself or herself. That, he suggests, is the only way to fully eliminate one's vulnerability to evil. His comments are worth careful evaluation and reflection.

At one point in the interview, he cried, as he thought about the disease and hardship of life in Africa—and the obstacles Africa must still overcome in reaching full status as a member of the world community. I was deeply impressed by the maturity of this man's compassion and tenderness. Indeed, throughout the whole interview, the room was charged with a special quality of reverence. At times, as he was speaking, he focused on specific elements of the quality of love, and the magnetic charge in the room intensified even more. Then, as he withdrew at the end of the session, he gave a silent benediction, which left us uplifted for the rest of the day.

As I understand it, that was the kind of person he was in the flesh as well. Like Jesus, he revealed the nature of spiritual love in all that he did—in what he said and wrote, through his acts, and by his attitudes and approach to life. The power of love was with him as he spoke; it filled him as he wrote. Indeed, I would highly recommmend any of his later writings.

In the interview, Dr. Schweitzer appears through

the mediumship of my good friend, David Kendrick Johnson. David was the medium for almost all of the interviews in the first series; he is a very gifted artist and psychic. Also participating in the interview was my colleague, Carl Japikse.

*Leichtman:* I'd like to start by discussing with you your philosophy of "reverence for life." Can you describe how that approach to living evolved? What events or steps in reasoning led you to this reverence for life?

*Schweitzer:* I suppose the most important factor is that I was—and am—natively religious. I am a spiritual person at heart. As a child growing up, I began examining a lot of the precepts and beliefs that were taught; and, in careful reading of the Bible, I came to the realization that these were not just ideas to accept and believe, but they also had to be practiced every day, in my attitudes and acts. So, I started practicing them, and that became, gradually, my "reverence for life."

*Leichtman:* You spent a long time in religious studies, and wrote several books on the lives of Jesus and Paul. As I looked into this, it became apparent that your thinking about Biblical concepts went through a tremendous evolution. Early on, you seemed to take a rather literal view of the life of Jesus and what He taught. Later on, your perspective seemed to become more of what I would call the "rational mystic." How did that evolution occur?

*Schweitzer:* A true mystic is always rational.

*Leichtman:* I should hope so.

*Schweitzer:* As you know, mysticism in not anti-intellectual. The impressions of the true mystic are just as rational as they are heartfelt. And to answer your question, I had a number of intuitive impressions about Jesus that gradually influenced my perspective. I guess you could say I had a vision of Him which changed my thinking drastically.

*Leichtman:* You had a vision of Him which changed your life?

*Schweitzer:* Yes—not in the sense of seeing an image of Him, but I did have a profound insight into His all-encompassing love and dedication. After that, I knew for sure He is a living presence of great importance. It is impossible to question His significance after an experience of that intensity. And it's probably also impossible *not* to have reverence for life after this kind of experience. Reverence for life is a very important aspect of Christianity. As you are wont to say, man has been put here to be God's steward on earth. I sincerely believe that.

*Leichtman:* In your early books, such as *The Search for the Historical Jesus*, you wrote of the kingdom of heaven as a supernatural kingdom to be experienced after death and the resurrection of the body. At that point, you apparently had not evolved the philosophy of life you held later on. How much of the difference between your early and later thinking is the result of the fact that the clergy of that day seemed unimaginative and literal-minded?

*Schweitzer:* A good deal of it. I had to accept some of the ideas of the clergy simply because I was monitored in my writing efforts.

*Leichtman:* Yes—as I remember it from your biographies, the mission society that sent you to Africa could accept you as a doctor but not as a minister, because your ideas were a bit too "radical" for them.

*Schweitzer:* That's true.

*Leichtman:* Well, many people in Christianity and other religions talk a great deal about "love," but never seem to express much love in their lives. You, by contrast, seemed impelled to demonstrate Christian charity.

*Schweitzer:* Yes, and I'll tell you why. The statement in the Bible, "By their acts ye shall know them," struck me as very important. To demonstrate love seemed far more significant than talking about it. It was an imperative to me. But it was sincere; I didn't expect to get a lot of "credit points" from my peers for being a loving person.

*Leichtman:* What was your attitude toward the clergy and philosophers of that day—your peers—who talked and talked about love but didn't really treat their fellow man with much affection, let alone love? How did you handle that paradox, that sanctimony? Did it embitter you or depress you?

*Schweitzer:* No—I did my best to demonstrate my views about love and reverence as vital aspects of religion, and tried to help them see that they were off the path a bit. You also have to remember that many people enter the ministry not because they are religious, but because it enables them to exercise a certain power over people they would not have otherwise. Unfortunately, that is a very common reason why people enter the ministry.

*Leichtman:* Yes, I'm aware of that. Well, why did you choose to go to Africa, of all places, to demonstrate the power of love? Why didn't you do your work in Europe, where life and circumstances would have been more comfortable and familiar?

*Schweitzer:* Well, for one thing, there was a greater need in Africa, and love responds best to a genuine need. The need itself drew me, in a way. Another factor was that I wanted to test myself a bit.

*Leichtman:* Well, you certainly did that.

*[Laughter.]*

*Schweitzer:* I should say so! It became apparent very quickly after I arrived that the clinical standards of Europe were just not going to work in the jungle. We found we had to be willing to sacrifice some of those clinical standards in order to make the people comfortable. Otherwise, they would not have come: they would not have been able to relate to a European-type hospital setting. They would have been frightened. Now, that was a real test, but we worked out ways so that the families could stay with the patient, as often as possible.

You know, I wish modern hospitals in Europe and America were more like that, permitting the family to stay with the patient. A hospital can be very frightening and depressing, and that can impede the process of getting well.

*Leichtman:* Wasn't there also a problem of superstition, which made it more desirable to let the family stay with the patient?

*Schweitzer:* Oh, yes. Some of the people, for example, would only eat food that had been cooked by their wife or a family member. Of course, that wasn't just superstition—they were also afraid of being poisoned by other patients!

We solved a lot of these problems by providing

dormitories for the patients and their families—a space in which they could build a hut and live in it together.

*Leichtman:* I want to return for a minute to our discussion of philosophy. During your life, you were impressed by and wrote about the problems of skepticism and pessimism in world philosophy and religion. Do you still see these as major problems?

*Schweitzer:* Absolutely—and they are both deadly to religion and philosophy. Pessimism and skepticism are really outpicturings of the blight of materialism, which blinds us to an inner view of life, so that all we can see are the difficulties of physical life and emotional impoverishment. The pessimist and skeptic are so busy being pessimistic and skeptical that they are unable to perceive spiritual values.

We live in an imperfect world. There's a lot wrong with society and with people—and it's discouraging. I would certainly be sympathetic with any intelligent person who does, from time to time, entertain pessimistic thoughts and feelings about his life, work, and society. When you read in books that God is love and hear people talk about how wonderful it is that God has designed the world and loves us, it is sometimes very challenging to your faith and intelligence to accept these ideas at face value, when there is so much disease, distress, pain, and misery in the world. Some doubt, skepticism, and pessimism is probably rational, because the problems to be solved are not easy ones. But what is absolutely irrational is the assumption that the problems *are all there is*, that the world is somehow dead or corrupt. It is irrational to assume we're doomed, that life is doomed, and society is doomed—that life is hell and is never going to get any better.

This is the great advantage that the people who find meaning in life and value in their religion, whatever it is, have over the pessimists and skeptics. They know there's something more than the problems and misery. This is particularly true in Christianity, and also in Judaism. We are supposed to look to God as a source of salvation—not salvation from fire and hell, but salvation from this blight of pessimism, depression, and misery.

*Japikse:* Salvation from our own negative attitudes.

*Schweitzer:* Yes, and from the attitudes of those around you. Bear in mind that I probably saw more misery, grief, and sickness in my lifetime than most people would see if they lived five hundred years. And when you confront that kind of misery, you can either kill yourself with agony and frustration and depression, or you can try, as best you can, to correct things and make life better. You try to be healing, soothing, and reassuring. And as you do, you align yourself with the forces of the world that are healing, soothing, and reassuring themselves. Pretty soon, you come to know that there *are* hidden resources of light and love, dignity and nobility in yourself, in other people, and in all creation.

As you continue to work with these forces, as your ally, they become very real to you. They prove their existence to you as you reach out for them—to get through another day, to rise above your fatigue, to conquer your pessimism, or to be helpful in the world, in whatever way you have the opportunity to do so. The misery, pessimism, or depression never go away entirely, but they eventually threaten you less, because you become absolutely convinced that your real identity, your real source of life and help, is the great universal force called God. This force is God's power, wisdom, love, and nobility all wrapped up together, permeating all life.

My point is this: the objective world is sometimes pretty miserable, sometimes very beautiful. But it is *designed* to be beautiful, lovely, and healthy—and *we* are designed to know that and appreciate it. And we have a duty to help others see this, too. We have the duty to work with God's wisdom and love to help make the world a better place in which to live and to be a healing influence in whatever we do in life, whether we are raising children or tending the sick or teaching school or working in a factory. We can all take on God's life as an ally in our daily life. In the beginning, we do this in order to find relief from our discontent, but eventually we do it to be more helpful in the world.

*Japikse:* How much of this pessimism and skepticism is a result of our own struggles with difficulty and grief, and how much is the result of contamination of theology and philosophy with ideas that focus us on doom, hell, and despair?

*Leichtman:* Yes, hasn't the church in particular been a major contributor to pessimism and skepticism?

*Schweitzer:* Of course it has. That's why the church is so attractive to those people who lust for the power to manipulate others. Think of it in this way: if you were brought up in a family filled with apathy, fear, depression, or discouragement, it would be very hard for you to overcome that conditioning. And it would be twice as difficult if you were also being told in church, with enthusiasm and in great detail, that you were born in sin, living in sin, sure to die in sin, and therefore going to hell.

There are agents of doom and gloom everywhere in society, and these people often attract quite a following. Human nature still contains a lot of fear and pettiness, and these charismatic individuals often prey on that ignorance and fear in society. At times, they become very influential. It's a terrible problem, and I don't have any great remedy for it, except this. Every person has an obligation to think for himself and to realize that no matter how rotten life may seem, or how much others may make of the hardships of living, there is also beauty in life. There is still love, affection, and goodwill in human nature. There are still moments in our life which fill us with joy and contentment. No one is without these moments, not even the Hitlers of the world.

So, each of us has a choice in this regard—a choice of whether we will feed on misery and hardship, or on the things of life which delight us and fill us with beauty, happiness, and peace.

The evidence of the beauty and joy of life is always present, even in the physical world, as imperfect as it is. Even in the jungle we could find it. Even in darkest Africa we could find evidence of God's light and love and beauty. It's in the people, it's in the country. It's not that difficult to find. But to find it, you must realize that the prophets of doom are wrong—dead wrong. And they ought to be ignored. As more people do this, they will fill the churches of the prophets of doom with emptiness—with the most lovely emptiness you can imagine. And that's just what the prophets of doom deserve.

*Leichtman:* Emptiness?

*Schweitzer:* Emptiness!

*Leichtman:* Is there a special responsibility on the part of those people who seek to serve humanity and God to guard against being pessimistic while they serve? Teachers, for example, have a marvelous opportunity to convey the healthy attitudes toward life you have described, but often just end up regurgitating the philosophy of pessimism.

*Schweitzer:* Well, I think your question answers itself. There is no doubt that we have an obligation to keep our misery to ourselves. It's a case of good manners and common sense; if you have a cold, you don't rush down to the store or restaurant and sneeze on everyone. So why would anyone want to sneeze the germs and viruses of his pessimism, anger, or fear on to anyone else?

Now, I'm very much aware that many good parents, teachers, and counselors feel the necessity of warning their children, students, or patients of their naivete and preparing them for the fact that the world is not a perfect place. That's not pessimism—that's just being realistic. But if they then go on and broadcast a message which basically indicates that there is no hope, no future, and that everyone is just as mean, hostile, and depressed as they are, then that's nonsense.

Actually, I suppose that's worse than sneezing—it's more the psychological equivalent of spreading the bubonic plague. Pessimism can be terribly infectious—and so can defeatism, cynicism, and anger. These are infectious plagues raging throughout society. Everyone ought to be aware of these plagues and protect himself from them—and from those people who carry them. This is a very serious problem, as serious as the Black Death of the Middle Ages. It's literally wiping out the useful lives of millions of people.

*Leichtman:* Yes, I know exactly what you mean—and I hope our readers won't be tempted just to dismiss it as a clever metaphor. You are not really using this as a metaphor at all, are you?

*Schweitzer:* No, I'm talking about something quite real. The plague of pessimism is just as real as trees and rocks and mountains. The forces of doubt, cynicism, despair, and anger probably do more to harm people than the pollution of the air and water and earth does, or an ailment such as tuberculosis.

*Leichtman:* Well, what can we do about it? What's the treatment?

*Schweitzer:* I've already pretty much described the treatment on an individual level: each person has to come to grips, all by himself, with his God and the inherent beauty and benevolence of life. I guess we could carry our analogy of sickness a step further; if you were physically ill, one way of restoring good health would be to get plenty of fresh air, sunshine, a good diet, and rest. The same is true in overcoming the plague of pessimism. Getting fresh air would mean getting away from people who are prophets of doom and pessimism, people who constantly try to drag you down to their level of pettiness, fear, and anger. The sunshine would be the light of the spirit, our inner light of wisdom and love. If everyone would learn to bathe in that, every day, that alone would solve a majority of ills in society. Getting a good diet would mean feeding yourself with good ideas, noble aspirations, confidence, and optimism. And plenty of rest would mean that we should stop exercising the bad thoughts, the pessimism, and the anger which make us miserable.

It's been my observation that people persist in evil because they are afraid to take the responsibility to do something better. They go on being evil because it has become a habit. So, to fully treat this problem, on a societal level, people must be taught that they do have a responsibility to function morally. That's not an easy assignment, but it can be demonstrated. And, it is hoped, the demonstration will inspire the right people.

*Leichtman:* Since you just mentioned the word "evil," perhaps we'd better define it before going any further. How would you define it?

*Schweitzer:* Well, it's not quite what most people think it is. Evil does exist in the world, but not in the form of an individualized devil who tries to tempt us or hold us back. It is constructed out of the individual and collective ignorance, pettiness, apathy, fear, and anger of the human race.

*Leichtman:* Can you explain how that happens?

*Schweitzer:* Quite simply, there are a lot of people who do not yet understand that they are spiritual beings. They become annoyed at the circumstances of their lives, and start to hate life, or fear it, or just sink into despair and apathy. They deny their spiritual heritage, and that's evil. And as they are generating their hatred, fear, and anger, they in fact create energies we would call "evil."

I somewhat object to the term "evil," because it has so many terrible connotations. I would rather just say that there exists human pettiness and ignorance. There is sickness in the mind and heart, as well as the body, of many people. But it is all correctable. It can all be healed.

When we look at evil from this perspective, we can see that it is possible to conquer it individually. We can find within us the sources of goodwill, peace, courage, and strength that we need to combat our individual ignorance, fear, anger, or pessimism. And, whether or not we think of ourselves as religious, it is the duty of each of us to find this capacity within ourselves and use it. We must not surrender to the negativity in our lives.

*Japikse:* Well, many people interpret what the Bible says about evil quite literally, that there is a devil. After all, Matthew reports that Jesus faced three temptations from the devil, who appeared to Him and spoke to Him. And when Jesus said, ''Get thee behind me, Satan,'' the devil cowered and went away. Is that the way it happened? Many people believe it is, but you seem to be implying that Jesus was perhaps confronting something more subtle than a gross and deformed caricature of evil.

*Schweitzer:* Most of the major events of the life of Jesus, as recorded in the Bible, actually did happen as described, or in close approximation. But some of the stories are also symbolic. The life of Jesus, as told in the Gospels, is really meant to represent the Odyssey of every spiritual aspirant. Jesus the man had to confront, quite painfully, every element of His own human pettiness, fear, and anger, and conquer it, until it was completely extinguished. He also had to conquer the same elements in His friends, His family, His enemies, and, to some extent, in mass consciousness. This is also something every spiritual aspirant must do—he has to learn to handle the pettiness, anger, and fear in mass consciousness. We can't just live out our lives quietly, cleaning up our own act, and believing merrily, for the rest of our lives, that we have done our work and now are saved.

*Leichtman:* We don't just ascend to seventh heaven and stay there? *[Laughter.]*

*Schweitzer:* No one does that, not even the Masters. That would be like assuming that a ten-year-old who took a bath and scrubbed up completely would never have to take another bath the rest of his life. *[Laughter.]* It's a silly idea. You have to work very hard to spiritualize the personality, so that your wisdom, compassion, goodwill, and courage dominate every element of your human nature and life expression. And as you work to do this, you will find that negative elements within yourself and within mass consciousness come to the surface, to create difficulty for you, in the form of temptation.

That's the sort of temptation Jesus was facing in the story in the Bible. He was facing the demonic elements within mass consciousness—a battle or temptation which is far more difficult to handle than when you are dealing with your personal pettiness alone. Of course, the spiritual aspirant does tend to deal with both levels of temptation—personal and collective—at the same time. After all, the collective anger of humanity feeds your own personal anger. So, as you begin to conquer your own anger, you also begin to immunize yourself and separate yourself from the collective anger of the masses. But it is the ultimate temptation of confronting the pettiness and ignorance of mass consciousness that the story in the Bible symbolically describes.

Of course, at clairvoyant levels, the collective anger, vindictiveness, and lust within mass consciousness frequently appear in dream-like images. These dream images or symbols can have a lot of power to them, and can appear to you in your dreams or meditations or moments of crisis. They are actually more commonly felt than seen. But Jesus was an excellent clairvoyant, and so He would be able to see these dream images of the evil of mass consciousness. He could speak to the dream image, and the dream image could speak to Him. That doesn't mean Satan is real—but he does exist at one level of perception as a dream symbol representing the evil of mass consciousness.

I don't want to get too esoteric here, but more people ought to realize that every human being has a subconscious, and every subconscious knows how to dream and create dream images. You don't have to be trained to do this—it's automatic. You're born with this dreaming mechanism. And mass consciousness is really the subconscious of the whole human race. So it is possible, in dreams and at other times, to encounter symbols of mass consciousness that can be quite powerful. They aren't real, but they can seem real when you dream them. Jesus was confronting some of these dream symbols from the subconscious of the human race.

*Japikse:* Based on what you just said, it seems to me that we should each be very careful how we use our imaginations and subconscious thoughts. It doesn't sound as though it would be very healthy to go around emphasizing our images of pettiness, anger, and the like. I'm thinking in particular about the fundamentalists who rant and rage about Satan and condemn just about everyone to hell.

*Schweitzer:* The people who rant and rave about the devil are feeding the problem, by building up the dream image of Satan. They are summoning the devil—and whether they love it or hate it doesn't make any difference. They are feeding it. And in some ways, they create devilish qualities and forces—which is, of course, completely unChristian.

Jesus did not appear on earth to warn us that the devil is going to get us. He came to say and demonstrate by His love and wisdom that God is here to help you—not that the devil is going to get you, but that God is here to help you. If you share your life and burdens with Him, you will find that help. And that's the message Jesus gave, over and over again, through what He said and how He lived His life.

*Leichtman:* I think it can be said that your life demonstrated that same message, too. Your life story is a very rich example of true Christian charity and humility. It is people like you who enrich humanity and teach us to be loving, in spite of great obstacles. But weren't you depressed at times?

*Schweitzer:* Oh God, yes. The amount of human misery I saw in Africa was immense. By and large, the Africans still are in a state of misery. We knew we could only treat a fraction of the problem. We could only help those we could reach—and that was depressing.

*Leichtman:* I asked that because some people seem

to think that to be a proper Christian, you must always be gleefully cheerful.

*Schweitzer:* A proper Christian regards the world as it is and responds appropriately. Certainly, when Christ saw misery, He often cried.

*Leichtman:* Yes.

*Schweitzer:* And then, if it was appropriate, He healed the person. A true Christian would respond to whatever conditions presented themselves, knowing that every circumstance is an opportunity to do God's work.

*Leichtman:* I take it the same maxim would apply to a good Jew, or a good Buddhist, or a good Moslem.

*Schweitzer:* Yes. The theme of loving service is universal.

*Leichtman:* In your writings, you also talked about the idea that everyone must ultimately find his or her own spirituality through "resignation."

*Schweitzer:* Yes—this is part of developing a proper relationship with God. Resignation is the act of giving yourself over to the work of God.

*Leichtman:* Just what is it you are resigning from?

*Schweitzer:* From the self-centered belief that "I am the only important person in the world." This is a very arrogant attitude.

*Leichtman:* Yes. The popular phrase for it is "looking out for number one."

*Schweitzer:* You also have to resign from the notion that it is possible to create your own personal reality, and that God has little or no influence in your life. That just isn't so, and if you believe that it is, then life will give you abundant experiences to prove you're wrong.

By resignation, I'm referring to the attitude which Jesus demonstrated over and over again: by myself, I can't do much, but with the Father, I can do all things. It's a resignation from personal egotism, from delusion and ignorance, and from despair and misery. It starts with the realization that you as an individual are important, you have responsibilities and make a difference in the world, but if you are ever going to be something significant, you will have to align yourself with your spirit. You will have to accept your spirit and work with it. That means resigning some of your arrogance, ignorance, and pettiness—and embracing a greater dimension of life, the God within you.

And that doesn't mean treating the personality as though it were nothing. I'm talking about beginning to see the personality in its true perspective, as a vehicle for spirit, rather than a thing that exists all by itself, all for itself.

*Leichtman:* In your writings, you mentioned that other people take a different view of resignation. Some Easterners, for example, go through the steps of resignation but end up being apathetic and withdrawn from the world—which you certainly were not.

*Schweitzer:* That attitude is not appropriate in the Western world, as you well know. It is completely inappropriate.

*Leichtman:* I do know that, but some people don't seem to get the message.

*Schweitzer:* Our role in the West, and especially in Christianity, is to go about our worldly duties, doing the things that need to be done. Now, that doesn't happen very often, but there are some people who heed the ideal.

*Leichtman:* Some people say, however, that the physical world is just an illusion. If you get caught up in it, you delay your spiritual progress. If you try to help out, it's just an ego trip, so let it go. What would you say to that?

*Schweitzer:* I'm sorry, would you repeat the question? There's a rather large audience of spirits in the room, and I was distracted by a comment that was being made over here. I don't know if you've noticed the crowd or not [clairvoyantly].

*Leichtman:* Yes, if it gets any larger, we're going to have to charge admission. *[Laughter.]*

*Japikse:* A little manna from heaven.

*Leichtman:* And they can't touch our chocolate chip cookies, either. They may sniff, but not chew. Did you have chocolate chip cookies in Africa?

*Schweitzer:* No.

*Leichtman:* It must have been a truly impoverished, primitive life without chocolate chip cookies.

*[Laughter.]*

*Japikse:* Talk about sacrifice! A true test of Christian dedication. *[Guffawing.]*

*Leichtman:* Well, to return to my question. There are some people who say yes, you should be resigned from the world—in the sense of ignoring it, because it doesn't amount to anything. It's just an illusion. Any effort to get caught up in that illusion would simply delay your spiritual progress. This is what I call spiritual nihilism. What do you think about it?

*Schweitzer:* It is an attempt to live a lie. It is not the duty of a Christian to ignore the world. The healthy Christian goes about the world doing whatever is needed to make it a better place, to help his fellow man. Sitting and meditating all day long, which I assume is what you are talking about, doesn't do any good at all. Unless meditation is accompanied by the effort to be useful in the world, it can actually cause the personality to become disconnected from the spirit. The person would eventually die and that would be the end of that—except that he would have to come right back and try again, until he learned the purposes of living in the physical plane.

*Leichtman:* You obviously see the physical plane, then, as an integral part of God's creation—

*Schweitzer:* Oh, yes!

*Leichtman:* Deserving our full and loving attention.

*Schweitzer:* I wonder how people can convince themselves otherwise.

*Leichtman [laughing]:* They have to work very hard at it. Well, from what you've been saying, it seems to me that you found the antidote to pessimism and nihilism in your philosophy of affirming life. This affirmation or reverence of life was obviously something that profoundly guided you every day. How can other people find or touch this realization?

*Schweitzer:* It comes by integrating the healthiness of your inner life with the circumstances and work to be done in your outer life.

*Leichtman:* Can you give some examples of that?

*Schweitzer:* Well, in working with my patients, for instance, I knew that whenever a cure actually occurred it was because I was holding something of the love of God in my inner life and focusing it into my work. The power of that love, focused through my daily activities, was the healing force, as much as anything else.

*Leichtman:* I will want to come back to that topic of nonphysical healing, but what other ways could an average person put his attention on the inner life as he goes about his daily work?

*Schweitzer:* A simple opportunity for the woman who's a wife or mother is to go about her daily tasks bathed in the realization that she is a focus for the love of God, and so she radiates that love throughout the house. Many women do this quite successfully—in fact, it's more common than many people believe. These women are not necessarily able to carry on a brilliant conversation; they may not be strikingly beautiful. But they seize the opportunities available to them to express the love of God.

*Leichtman:* What kind of opportunities do the executive, the office worker, or the sales clerk have to do this?

*Schweitzer:* Well, the executive could focus love—I'm using this one aspect of God to make it simpler to talk about, but there are other aspects of the inner life—by letting his employees know that he is grateful for the work they do. He could express his appreciation every time someone does extra work, or does a job especially well, and he could take care not to fuss inappropriately about shortcomings in the performance of a job. The person working in the office can learn to love what he is doing and do the best job he can.

*Leichtman:* You're talking about doing something more than just being nice, aren't you?

*Schweitzer:* I'm talking about rising above the personality and contacting something of the inner life of the spirit, and then expressing that in your daily activities. Some people do assume that being nice is the same as being spiritual, but that's not usually the case. Niceness is generally just an expression of the pleasant elements of the personality. The life of spirit is something more.

If you really want to bring through the spirit, I would suggest a very simple technique. You should examine your life, your lifestyle, your friends, and the experiences of your life, and find as much as you can that is beautiful or noble or worthy of praise. Then, you should be deeply thankful that at least a fragment of God's kindness or goodness or nobility or beauty exists within you or your life experience. The evidence of this might be the kindnesses a co-worker has shown you, or the fact that your children are sometimes delightful and sweet, or the fact that you have done an exceptionally fine piece of work. But whatever it is, you should appreciate it, because it is good. You should thank God that this goodness exists, that this much of the inner life is being expressed, and it touches you. And it's marvelous.

At that point, you should also be thankful that something exists within the universe which makes this possible. And wouldn't it be great if this Something could dominate our lives, our experiences, our memories, and our future? If you practice this kind of thankfulness, you will actually begin to tap the hidden current of love behind all creation, all events, and all people. Just in talking about it now, I am tapping that current. It's very real for me—and it was very real for me much of my adult life in the physical plane.

Once you plug into this dimension of creation, everything else begins to come with it—guidance, power, courage, strength, healing, a glimpse of nobility, and even a glimpse of perfection. You get caught up in a state of mind and feeling that alters your whole perspective about yourself, your work, and the other people you know. For me, this is a complete formula for finding God within life and within ourselves—and for using it in daily life.

*Japikse:* Yet doesn't one have to do more than just believe in this current of love? You say you are tapping into it right now, and did so during your life as Albert Schweitzer. But I imagine there are a lot of readers who have never had this experience.

*Schweitzer:* That's why the practice of thankfulness is so important. Belief and faith are important—I don't want to say anything that would tarnish the value of right faith and right belief. But it is through thankfulness and praise that you begin to discover the inner presence of the God you propose to believe in. The only way you can link yourself to the power, love, and wisdom of God is by finding aspects of these qualities within yourself—within your mind and within your heart. And the easiest way to do that is by being thankful for whatever you can find that is worthy of being praised.

Now, this is really very easy to do. Even a child can do it—in fact, even a cat or a dog can be thankful. And so can every adult. Which means that every adult has the ability to focus something of God's will or God's plan into his life.

*Leichtman:* I think those are very important statements for people to muse about. Now, in addition to love, you wrote about the *will to love* and the *will to life*, which go beyond just loving people through your work. Could you define the will to love and the will to life in practical terms as well? The reason I'm asking is that there are so many people who think they can substitute emotional mushiness and sentimentality for spiritual love.

*Schweitzer:* Mushiness and sentimentality tend to indicate negative traits of emotional behavior, not love. They clutter up the emotions. No truly religious person would want to indulge in either mushiness or sentimentality: they are inappropriate to the life of spirit. A person who does this needs to be shown how to refocus on his inner life.

Now, to comment on the will to love and the will to life, the will to love, I suppose, is the power to act in a loving way. It is the power to do things which make you helpful and useful in the world, and that is categorically and dynamically different from love itself.

The person who never rises above sentimentality shortchanges himself, by thinking that's all there is. It's a whole lot better than being angry or miserable, I'll grant you, but it's certainly not all that love is meant to be.

You can sit in your bedroom or meditation room or cave or chapel and just love the world, but that may not be terribly helpful in dealing with very real human needs in society—or even your own family. People have to act; they have to do things. We live in the physical world and there are physical needs which have to be attended to, in physical ways. We have to use our hands and feet and mouths and typewriters and tape recorders. The will to love, then, is the power to act in a loving way. It's more than just love, and I wish more people would appreciate that. We are not doing our spiritual duty unless we ground our love in loving and healing activities.

Now, the will to life is a bit greater than the will to love, because life is more than just love. The will to life involves the expression of all aspects of one's livingness, and that would include the expression of talent, wisdom, intelligence, and life's purpose. It's quite different from the will to love. I'm tuning into it right now and am summoning these energies. It's qualitatively a different experience—a different vibration, if you will. In mundane terms, I suppose you would say the will to life is the impulse to use whatever you have in the way of talent or goodwill or good ideas to honor your opportunities and duties in life.

*Japikse:* When you say you are tuning into the will to love or the will to life, what do you mean? Where are these things located? Are you tuning into Mars, where there is a special repository of divine qualities, or how are you doing this?

*Schweitzer:* No, I'm tuning into the higher dimensions of my own self.

*Japikse:* By that, do you mean your own self, as opposed to the medium's self?

*Schweitzer:* Yes. But he has them, too.

*Japikse:* Sure.

*Schweitzer:* You find them within you. You can find them within every human being, but you have to rise to a dimension of spirit which Jesus poetically referred to as the kingdom of heaven. And the kingdom of heaven really is within. I don't know how people can miss the significance and implications of that message. It's so abundantly clear to me. The kingdom of heaven is an intense personal experience for me; it eradicates all doubt or cynicism about this topic.

I find it very frustrating that I can't go around giving this inner knowledge to others. Of course, this is the limitation on all teachers, gurus, and priests, and anyone else who is trying to talk about the kingdom of heaven and God's love and will. All of these things exist within each one of us, but none of them can ever be demonstrated with machines or gadgets. People can't take photographs of me and prove that the kingdom of heaven exists within me, and yet it's there. It's the most real thing that I experience. And it's the most real thing anyone else can experience, too. But that's the point: each person must find it for himself or herself. Each person must prove it to himself or herself through his or her own experience. Each person has to individualize and internalize this life of God. You can't get it out of a book. You can't get it by listening to me. I can only say that it does exist. It's marvelous. You can discover it, too, by following these steps.

It's not within your subconscious, or your pineal gland, or your solar plexus. It's within the dimension of your spirit. Everyone has one. So look for it there—in the essence of your own greatness and humanity, nobility and wisdom. No matter how long it takes or how difficult it may be, looking for it is exceedingly worthwhile.

*Leichtman:* How often, in your moments of fatigue and discouragement, did you feel that you were somehow being sustained or driven by a supernatural or transpersonal force?

*Schweitzer:* I felt that I was moved by that transpersonal force most of the time.

*Leichtman:* Would that kind of awareness be one

way of sensing the meaning of the will to love or the will to life—that there really is something within you that emanates from beyond your own personal desires and capacities?

*Schweitzer:* Certainly. Our most significant discoveries about life generally don't come in visions or while reading religious tracts; they come in simple insights gained in the midst of our daily activities. They come while we try to act in loving and kind ways.

*Leichtman:* Can we comment more on the idea of reverence for life? You wrote extensively about the need, in this regard, for every intelligent person to develop a system of rational ethics. How should the average person go about that? I take it from reading about you that you were rather against the notion of people allowing others to impose their dogma on them, accepting it as a matter of faith.

*Schweitzer:* Yes, this is the danger of unintelligent, blind belief. Now, I'm not trying to encourage cynicism and skepticism, which perpetuate ignorance as much as blind belief. Both extremes are antispiritual—they indicate that the person is surrendering his obligation to think. He's trying to avoid his responsibility to make critical decisions about his life. I'm talking about the decisions of ethics, of how he hopes to act. I'm talking about answering questions such as: ''What do I stand for?'' ''What do I accept as right in my life?'' ''What do I cherish as my ideals for living?''

As children, we naturally imitate the ethics of those who are very close to us, but as we become adults we must begin to revise our ethics in order to honor our own individuality and intelligence. We must become discerning about what is going on in life and make decisions and choices of our own.

Obviously, every person is going to make a lot of mistakes, but part of developing a code of ethics is being willing to make those mistakes, and learn from them. Any mistakes we may happen to make can be changed in due time. But at least they are *our* mistakes, and not someone else's we are just copying.

It's absolutely essential to do this for ourselves. If we are to avoid being passive victims of mass consciousness and the manipulations of other people, we must exercise our responsibility to think for ourselves. We must honor our duty to challenge, in gentle ways, the status quo, mass thought, and mass attitude. And we can do this without becoming arrogant or a rabble rouser. We can do it rationally, intelligently, and gently.

The basis for our ethics is meant to be our spiritual guidance. Our personal ethics are meant to reflect the spiritual wisdom and natural laws of the cosmos.

*Leichtman:* Well, what does that mean? I know some people who could take that last statement you made and interpret spiritual guidance to be whatever they feel they want to do.

*Schweitzer:* That's absolute nonsense. That's no basis for ethical living.

*Leichtman:* Well, what would you tell these people?

*Schweitzer:* I would tell them to ask themselves how they would want to be treated by life and by people—and then ask themselves, can I behave that way myself? Can I treat other people the way I would like them to treat me? If not, then they'd better revise their expectations of how others should treat them—

or vice versa.

*Leichtman:* It sounds like the Golden Rule.

*Schweitzer:* It is. And it's an excellent criterion for refining your ethics.

Another good guideline to use is the notion that God gave me my life. He also gave you your life. So, in a sense, we are both something of God, and in that light, we should treat each other ethically and with respect. We should not try to cheat each other, because we would be cheating God, and therefore ourself, because we are of God.

Now, I won't pretend that it can't be a real problem to try to understand how to act in specific circumstances. But that's the value of ethics—it gives us a framework for acting.

Ultimately, you become aware that there is an underlying, absolute truth to living—and that absolute truth is the life of God. Now, that's a long way from the notion of "doing anything you want." And it's also a long way from the rebellious attitude of, "No, I'm not going to listen to what anyone wants me to do—even God."

Part of the confusion surrounding ethics is a result of this. There's a natural tendency to let others make your decisions for you—and also a natural tendency to resist outside influences. Both of these tendencies are dangerous and must be outgrown. We must learn to think for ourselves. From time to time there may be unusual people that we admire and respect, and we may want to imitate them. Perhaps their advice is good for us, and so we accept it. But we have to be very selective in doing that, and make sure we have thoroughly evaluated it for ourselves.

*Japikse:* What you seem to be advocating here is not a collection of rules about what to do or what not to do, but a set of very active, living principles that can be applied to the circumstances of life. Is that a fair conclusion?

*Schweitzer:* I think so. Ethics have no use unless we can apply them to our lives. At times, of course, we may only be able to apply them in part. Our ethics are meant to be ideals for acting in life—if we could honestly do our very best, this is how we would like to treat others, and how we would like them to treat us. But even though we are often able to carry out these ethics, some days it's just not possible. We're tired or grumpy or have just gone through some tragedy. The fact that elements of our pettiness occasionally take over does not reduce the value of our ethics. So, within this context, yes, ethics are meant to be very active, living principles. If you simply sat around on a stump and speculated on what *could* be done and what other people *ought* to be doing, that would be nothing more than an exercise in sophistry and sanctimony.

The pursuit of a spiritualized set of ethics is really the effort to find God within you. You are trying to internalize God in your personality, in your life. You are trying to internalize your religion, by making conscious choices of your own. You hope that these choices are governed by your highest intelligence, and not by expediency, or by inflammatory articles in the newspaper, or the latest news on TV. As a general rule, they'll probably be consistent with the commonly-accepted ethics of religion, and sane, intelligent living. What I'm saying is that the pursuit of ethics is not going to make you an iconoclast, a hermit, an anti-establishment hippie. The rational development of ethics leads you back to God.

*Japikse:* Most people seem to think of God as something static, yet you seem to be implying that God is very active.

*Schweitzer:* Quite active, yes. And abundantly available, too, I might say.

*Leichtman:* This seems to be a point where you differed from the standard philosophy and theology of your day. The philosophers and theologians of your time tended to see God, and many still do, as the abstract, invisible essence of life.

*Schweitzer:* Who was somewhere up in the sky.

*Leichtman:* Yes—remote, aloof, unavailable, and perhaps indifferent.

*Schweitzer:* Well, life just does not work that way. I think of God as being everywhere. I have had this proven to myself on many occasions. When I can cover myself with God's love and then heal someone, I have proof.

*Leichtman:* Yes, I understand. You are thinking of God as a very active, vital force in the midst of daily life.

*Schweitzer:* And He is always right there—before you, within you, and everywhere around you.

*Japikse:* It seemed to me in reading about you that you considered the realization of the active nature of God to be almost a prerequisite of spiritual resignation. A lot of people resign themselves or sacrifice themselves, but without having that kind of commitment to an active expression of the life of God.

*Schweitzer:* Yes, and without that dedication, it's obviously a false resignation.

*Japikse:* They are resigning to something other than God.

*Schweitzer:* They are going through the motions of a formula they really don't understand, in the hopes of becoming immediately more aware. But a false resignation does not bring an expansion of consciousness. It might bring the semblance of growth, but it would only last a short while.

*Leichtman:* What about the people who try to find God by entering a passive, mentally numb state of mind?

*Schweitzer:* That doesn't work, either. It's a type of false resignation, because you have to work actively and earnestly. You have to express the love and wisdom of God to find the love and wisdom of God.

*Leichtman:* You mean you can't just ''be,'' as they say, and find God?

*Schweitzer:* That's right.

*Leichtman:* You seemed to promote an almost revolutionary concept for theologians: that we should not accept our religious beliefs simply on the basis of faith. We need to look for the evidence which will add understanding to our belief.

*Schweitzer:* I remember having the awareness quite early in life that the concepts taught by theologians now are not the ideas Christ intended to teach. He worked very hard to attain His gifts of spirit—and He worked hard to use them in a mature, loving way.

The major obligation of religion in the West is to help people find an element of God in themselves and in their lives. Religion should provide instruction in how to do this and assist people in healing those aspects of their lives which need a touch of the divine—a touch of guidance, inspiration, love or whatever. Churches should do this for society as a whole, too, at least to some extent.

And here's something interesting to think about: the reason that many theologians have become political—and it really is appropriate for them—is that they have tried to find God and have failed, for one reason or another.

Religion runs into problems when it starts imposing rules and regulations, instead of inspiring people to discover the kingdom of heaven within themselves. That substitutes faith in dogma for faith in the Christ, faith in the benevolence of life itself. And it gradually distorts the emphasis of the church and its theology, from spiritual to political. As a result, an occasional individual may be attracted to the ministry for the wrong reasons—for the comfort of a powerful position in the community and the opportunity to control people, rather than help them. It's unfortunate that this occurs, but these people are fairly easy to spot. They do not have the basic reverence for life.

I think I've wandered off the topic somewhat.

*Leichtman [chuckling]:* You're allowed to do that. I was asking, I suppose, about the anti-intellectual aspect of the modern church. There are some people, for example, who claim that all you have to do to be a properly spiritual person is read the Holy Scriptures and believe them. They advocate accepting spiritual values and ideals on faith alone, and regard intelligent inquiry as a sign of weakness of faith. Some of these people, for instance, would say that there is no need to bother to research the phenomena of life after death; you should accept this on faith alone.

*Schweitzer:* Well, I don't want to say anything that could be construed as antifaith, because faith is important. But the proper Christian also understands that the mind is important, and must not be negated. The proper Christian doesn't just read the Scriptures and believe them; he thinks about them. Now, that doesn't mean that he questions whether they are right or not; it means he thinks about how this passage of Scripture can help him, in his daily life. What does it tell him about the inner life of God—and about expressing that inner life in his life? The Scriptures were written to lead you to the kingdom of heaven, but you have to do your share of hard work, too. And that requires the active use of the mind and intellect.

*Leichtman:* Yes, it's a tremendous challenge to anyone's mind to approach subjects as profound and vast as God and mysticism and the nature of life. Where should one begin? How do we know we're making progress?

*Schweitzer:* Well, one sign that you're making progress is that the Scriptures begin to have greater meaning for you. They're not just something to believe anymore; they also have personal meaning and application to you. They come alive in your life, and help you improve the quality of your life and work. You become more aware of the beauty around you, and view the things that are ugly from a higher perspective. There are many signs of progress which can be observed, but most of them are very ordinary. Your attitudes toward the events of life become more mature; your dealings with others become more harmonious. Your work becomes more inspired. Your reverence for life deepens.

Now, as for where to begin, I think I've already covered that. You begin by looking within, and finding the sparks of divinity already at work in your life. That's much more important than memorizing the Bible, so that you can quote chapter and verse better than anyone else, and win every argument. The Bible was not written for the purpose of hitting other people over the head with it—either figuratively or literally. *[Laughter.]* It was written to guide us and inspire us in our thinking. *It is meant to be thought about!* And if the person who memorizes the Bible would spend as much time thinking about it as he does committing it to memory, he would know a lot more than chapter and verse.

*Leichtman:* I'd like to talk some more about Africa, if we might. You obviously found great meaning in the work you did in Africa. How did that evolve over the many decades you lived and labored there?

*Schweitzer:* Well, the greatest source of meaning lay in the opportunities I had to help people. That started with helping the people become healthier, but it included a lot more, too. I was able to help them deal with their problems more intelligently and less superstitiously, for example. We were also able to help some of the young people become citizens of the twentieth century, and that was the beginning of something we hoped would continue. That would be the process of helping Africa become a citizen of the twentieth century. I suppose that would be one of the greater purposes of the work I tried to do.

Right now, there are many clumsy attempts going on to make Africa a fuller citizen of the twentieth century. Many of them won't work—especially the ex-

[61]

periments in socialism. I don't see how people can advocate any style of socialism; it just won't work in the world.

*Japikse:* Why not?

*Leichtman:* Yes, why not?

*Schweitzer:* The citizen in a socialist country spends his life living under someone else's authority and responsibility. He is not responsible for doing his own work or making his own way—the state is. And that is antispiritual. Socialism is antispiritual by nature, whether or not religion is banned, because it dehumanizes the individual. It dehumanizes society. All of life becomes a bureaucracy in a socialist country.

*Leichtman:* What about Marxism?

*Schweitzer:* I'm including Marxism as a brand of socialism, but I'm talking about more than just communism. I'm including the whole socialist movement. At one time, in Europe, some of the basic principles and ideals of socialism could have done some good—if they had been applied differently. But as it is now, socialism is so horribly dehumanizing that I don't think it is possible to rationally defend it.

*Leichtman:* What do you think the outcome of all this will be?

*Schweitzer:* By and large, Africa will become a democratic continent—eventually.

*Leichtman:* That must be a long ways in the future. I see no sign of it, as yet.

*Schweitzer:* It might make it by the next century. I don't really know when this will happen, but it is already beginning to occur—in very small ways, to be sure, but it is beginning. The Africans are beginning to realize that they want to be free to be the best people they can be. And they are being taught to think in that way by a few people here and there. Certainly, that's something we tried to teach the people who came to us. We tried to teach them the value of bettering their life and the value of helping one another.

*Leichtman:* Well, it only makes sense that if our Creator designed us to be free, within reason, to be helpful to one another, and to be proper stewards of the earth, then that intention should eventually have some influence on the nature of our governments and social institutions.

*Schweitzer:* Absolutely. And it has had its impact, perhaps more than many people realize. America would be one example. This country is more fortunate than most, in that you have the latitude to do your own work, to be a good person, and to be a helpful person. There may be times when it seems that you are helplessly bound in the regulations of government, but the system does have within it the mechanism to right itself eventually. And, I'm told, there is going to be some "housecleaning" in your government that will really take. The citizens are tired of being ashamed of being Americans, and that apparently will be the impetus for some effective reforms.

*Leichtman:* Ah, so we don't have to move to Canada, after all. *[Laughter.]*

I had a professor in medical school who had worked with you in Africa. He was a red-faced, chubby Austrian named Zeller.

*Schweitzer:* Oh, yes, I remember him.

*Leichtman:* He was a very kind fellow, but very discouraged about his work in Africa, as if the vastness of the medical needs, and the primitive and superstitious nature of the natives, made the work almost impossible. His attitude was that his contribution was negligible.

*Schweitzer:* But the people he helped, he did help.

*Leichtman:* Of course.

*Schweitzer:* Well, it's important to keep that in focus. And it's also useful to have ways to renew yourself, so that you don't get overwhelmed by such attitudes. In my case, being able to play the organ served the purpose of reestablishing my perspective toward my work. Through the music I played, I was also able to do a little meditating, and that renewed me, too.

I was very discouraged the first few years I was in Africa. At one time or another, the fact that we could do so little was very discouraging to all of us. But I tried to handle it by simply thinking about the person I happened to be treating right then. I disciplined myself to think about helping him get well, and then I went on to the next. I found that much more effective than dwelling on all the masses of people who were sick in Africa. Sometimes, you have to be pragmatic in order to preserve your sanity.

*Leichtman:* That would seem to be a good guideline for anyone seeking to serve God: to keep focused on the practical things we can do, instead of worrying about the vastness of human needs.

*Japikse:* To pursue the good we can do, and not the good we cannot do.

*Schweitzer:* I'd like to share a memory here. I remember being very depressed late one afternoon, so I went to a place on the grounds where I liked to walk at that time of the evening, if I had the time, because the shadows of the late sun through the leaves of the trees always fascinated me. And just as I turned the corner of the building to go there, to watch and wonder, I saw two little black children playing together, having such a good time. They were dancing and playing in the sunlight that I also loved so much. And I thought, isn't it wonderful that these two children, surrounded by all this misery, can have such a good time? And I immediately felt better. I kept the memory of that evening in my mind ever after that, so that whenever I became depressed, I could think about it and the joy of that particular moment of time. And that would refresh me and help me go on.

*Leichtman:* I suppose we all have to find these magical moments.

*Schweitzer:* What I was taken with was the absolute beauty of those two innocent children, and their playing, and the sunlight through the trees. I was thankful for being able to see such beauty, and that made me feel better.

*Leichtman:* I suppose that's what you meant when you said that the best evidence of God's love and God's beauty here on earth is found in ordinary moments.

*Schweitzer:* Yes.

*Leichtman:* Did your music also have that reassuring, inspiring effect on you?

*Schweitzer:* Of course. I loved the times I could get away for a little while to play the organ. But I played music primarily because it was extremely enjoyable to me. I felt marvelous. And it did have a healing effect on me—and even on the other people in the compound. The organ could be heard almost everywhere in the compound, and it seemed to have a calming effect, even on the people who didn't understand the music. But that wasn't the reason why I played the music. I played because I found joy and beauty in it, and was delighted to give a sense of joy and beauty to those who might be listening.

I must confess that playing music was such a natural thing for me that I never even thought about why I was doing it. It's like eating; you don't have to have an intellectual reason for eating. You get hungry and you eat. There's no big mystery about it. It's a natural thing, and playing music was as natural to me as eating. I wish more people would appreciate that it's not always necessary to analyze everything they do and produce an elaborate set of reasons justifying it. Sometimes you do a helpful, healthy thing just because it's natural to do it; you would never think of *not* doing it. This is often especially true when the spirit dominates the personality. The personality starts doing things that are simply natural to the life of spirit.

In playing music, I found a sense of beauty and joy that lifted up my spirits. I was also very much aware at times that this sense spread to others listening to the music—even those who weren't paying attention to it. It was easiest to see the effect on children, but it sometimes even influenced the animals. So, I kept it up.

Of course, from my current perspective, I can see that music does have a healing impact. Certain kinds of good music—particularly Bach—have a tremendous tranquilizing and healing impact on the emotions, and to some extent, the mind. When the emotions are calm and the mind is focused on the lofty qualities of life, such as joy, goodwill, and beauty, then all healing channels are nourished. The healing qualities of music can have their most direct impact on the personality, but indirectly they can also heal the physical body.

*Leichtman:* You were a recognized authority on Bach. Of all composers, why did Bach seem to strike your fancy so much?

*Schweitzer:* When I was playing Bach, I found God in the midst of the music. It was a very real, joyous experience for me. I found God's love and peace and order and wholeness while playing Bach. I became consumed in my spirit. Now, I realize that not everyone who listens to Bach, or even plays Bach, has this same experience. But it is potentially there for everyone.

*Japikse:* Would you care to comment on specific qualities of spirit which might be focused through Bach's music?

*Schweitzer:* Well, I probably should leave a question of that nature to Richard Wagner [whose interview will appear later in *From Heaven to Earth*].

*Leichtman:* Oh, we'll ask him, too, but you might have a better feel for Bach.

*Schweitzer:* Well, let's see. First, we'd better specify which Bach we're talking about. I will limit myself to Johann Sebastian Bach, and not his relatives. Now, Bach wrote in many different styles. But to give you a simple answer, the music of Bach tends to be very compatible with the theme of reverence for life and devotion to ideals, which I suppose is why I was in such harmony with it.

Whenever I played Bach, the music filled me with the awareness and conviction that there is something within every person, every animal, every plant, and every element of life that is utterly lovely and beautiful. I was filled with awe and reverence and devotion. Some aspects of Bach are more focused in joyfulness, but the overall effect of Bach's music tends to create a genuine sense of sympathy. There's a consoling, reassuring, mystical presence in his music.

Other aspects of Bach's music contain the kind of refinement you find in highly organized, carefully structured intelligence. There's a sense of refinement in Chopin's music, too, but it's different. In Bach, it is the refinement of a meticulously conceived plan—as though it were part of a divine engineering work connecting heaven with earth. It helps tune the listener into the intelligence and mind of God.

The curious thing is that these qualities of Bach will tend to draw an appropriate response even from people who do not understand the music.

*Leichtman:* That's not surprising. After all, music speaks directly to the subconscious.

I'd like to talk about Africa some more. What can you tell us about the types of illnesses you encountered there? Certainly, they would be quite different in Africa than what we are accustomed to here in the West. What special problems did you have in dealing with these illnesses?

*Schweitzer:* The problem of infections was a great deal more serious in Africa than it would be here. We lost a great number of people to some simple infections that don't even affect Westerners. We tried inoculating everyone who came to us to try to prevent these infections, but we didn't always have enough serum.

Many of the people who came to us had wounds of one sort or another, but we were also able to spot other problems and correct them while they were staying with us.

*Leichtman:* You did a lot of surgery, too, didn't you?

*Schweitzer:* Yes. I would do more amputations in a year than I ever thought one doctor would see in a lifetime—and mind you I had to work in conditions that were somewhat less favorable than a modern hospital.

*Leichtman:* Why amputations?

*Schweitzer:* A person would get a cut on the foot, for instance, but by the time he had reached our hospital, it was so infected that the leg had to be removed. Gangrene was a big problem.

*Leichtman:* You recorded that there were many strangulated hernias, also.

*Schweitzer:* Yes.

*Leichtman:* Did you find much mental illness in "stress-free" Africa?

*Schweitzer:* Ohhh—particularly in women.

*Leichtman:* Really!

*Schweitzer:* Most of the time, we could do very little to help them.

*Leichtman:* How was the mental illness you saw in Africa different from what we deal with here?

*Schweitzer:* A lot of it was based on the fact that the typical African is very superstitious. I ran into a lot of people who thought they were possessed by a demon. Because they believed it, in effect, they were. It was very difficult to deal with those people. For one thing, just communicating with them could be quite a problem. But we tried everything—we even found a couple of witch doctors to help us deal with many of these patients. They would communicate more readily with the witch doctor. And the one we used the most was intelligent enough to know that I was trying to help these people, so he cooperated.

*Leichtman:* Was witchcraft a prevalent problem?

*Schweitzer:* It was almost universally practiced, in one form or another. I'm not saying that everyone was a witch doctor, but everyone at least had amulets somewhere on him. Many of the men would carry around medicine bags, very much like the American Indians.

*Leichtman:* Was this responsible for a significant amount of the mental illness you encountered—or was it just a harmless superstition most of the time?

*Schweitzer:* Well, some of the mental illness was caused by the sheer hardship of life in Africa, of course. Women would commonly get terribly depressed and become catatonic, simply because of the enormous burden they had to carry all the time. But, yes, superstition was a major factor—and certainly not harmless.

Superstition is a terrible problem in Africa and other underdeveloped areas where the culture is not especially advanced. Of course, superstition exists in some of the most sophisticated areas of Western civilization, too, but it takes a different form. Human nature tends to think in magical terms—we project our feelings and ideas and personalize the meaning of events. We will react to a simple event in which someone annoys us by magnifying its meaning to us—by assuming, for example, that this one event is proof of the individual's deep dislike for us. That's superstition—and we all tend to do this, from time to time.

When you are dealing with a more unsophisticated group of individuals, such as the natives of Africa, this kind of magical thinking becomes very active. The natural fears of these people and their lack of understanding combine to make superstition a very, very powerful force indeed. And while human nature has its beautiful side, it also has its ugly side, and an awful lot of anger, rage, defensiveness, and possessiveness get expressed. And that's more threatening than the beautiful, so the average person tends to be more obsessed by it. Then, in Africa, you have to add another factor: that the simple survival involved in just getting through the day or growing up to adulthood tends to consume the bulk of a person's attention. If you're confronted on a daily basis by the raw, destructive forces of nature and the literal beasts of the jungle, it's not too surprising that sometimes you might have to confront nonphysical beasts. The African native often lives in a jungle of his fears and superstitions, as well as the physical jungle—a cultural and psychological environment of focused negativity, possessiveness, jealousy, fear, and so on. Because of the proclivity to magical thinking, these emotions tend to take on symbolic form, and terrible things are created in the collective feeling and traditions of the tribes.

I can look back on this problem and see it more clearly now. And, yes, these collective fears and angry forces can be used to harm people, when manipulated by evil people. It does happen.

The African tribesmen simply don't know any

better. They live that way and they die that way. I'm not condemning them. But a good deal of illness was generated as a result of these problems. It was usually triggered by jealousy or fear between two people, or an argument between two families, caused by some social gaffe. It was very common to seek revenge by means of magic.

There wasn't much we could do about these illnesses, because they were more psychological than physical. We did try to reassure the patients that they were under our protection and had nothing to fear; we tried to immunize them from their own superstition and environment, but it wasn't terribly effective.

*Leichtman:* Well, these problems are difficult to treat even today, with our modern facilities and training. They must have been even more difficult for you in Africa. Let me move on to a different aspect of the medical work: what we today call faith healing or spiritual healing. Did you consider this a significant part of your work?

*Schweitzer:* Certainly. As I said earlier, it was my loving concern as much as my medical treatments that helped the men and women I treated become well—and I fully believed that during my lifetime, too. We tried to create an environment of health, an environment of love at the compound. Whenever possible, for example, we tried to give some of the people who came to us positions in the compound, in order to help them keep the quality of their life a little better than it had been. It also relieved us of some of the burdens of routine work. We didn't really pay them, but gave them a place to live and food to eat, and saw to it that the quality of their life improved.

What I am saying is that we didn't just treat them, we *cared* about them.

*Leichtman:* Did you ever go so far as to practice "laying on of hands"?

*Schweitzer:* Of course.

*Leichtman:* I bet you even prayed for your patients. *[Laughter.]*

*Schweitzer:* Absolutely. I take my religion seriously—now, even more seriously than before.

*Leichtman:* Spiritual healing, laying on of hands, and that kind of thing are becoming very popular nowadays.

*Schweitzer:* Yes, but people ought to be very careful about seeking out this kind of healing.

*Leichtman:* Why is that?

*Schweitzer:* When you are being healed by laying on of hands, you are picking up elements of the consciousness of the person doing the healing. As you know, not all of the people who practice this kind of healing are virtuous and filled with the reverence for life. Some are not even particularly good people. If that's the case, then the "healer" would leave you with something very undesirable—something much worse than what you had to begin with.

*Leichtman:* Then that would be a "sicker" instead of a "healer." *[Groaning.]*

Is spiritual healing something that should be talked about and perhaps taught in medical schools?

*Schweitzer:* Definitely. And I'm delighted to see that more and more medical people are giving it more attention, and finding it to be helpful. Spiritual healing, after all, is a natural companion to the scientific techniques used by the average physician in his daily practice. It doesn't replace them, but neither should medicine replace the spiritual side of healing. They ought to complement each other.

Frankly, I would be very concerned about anyone entering the profession of medicine, psychology, or nursing who rejected the concept of spiritual healing. I'm not saying doctors and nurses should necessarily practice laying on of hands, but I think it is stunning if they reject the possibility of spiritual healing. It is always the spirit that does the healing. Medicine is a set of practices which augment that healing process. Every physician, psychologist, and nurse ought to understand that he or she is only able to act with full effectiveness when cooperating with the spirit of the patient.

Spiritual healing is not the exclusive property of grim-faced clerics, after all. Deep within each person is a healing force which every health professional needs to understand is his ally. It is there to be summoned, and applied. It can be fed by our own reverence and appreciation of it. It can be nurtured by our prayers. *These* are the practices of spiritual healing.

*Japikse:* From these remarks, and the comments you made earlier about superstition, it would seem to me that spiritual healing is really the direct antithesis of superstition. Superstition can only occur in the absence of spirit, whereas spiritual healing calls in the presence of spirit. I mention this because many people seem to think of spiritual healing as superstition.

*Schweitzer:* Yes, I think you have a valid point. The basic power of superstition is fear and ignorance; its net effect is to destroy. In spiritual healing, however, you are dealing with different forces, in a different dimension, with a different purpose, and different results. The only thing the two have in common is that both require a certain measure of belief. But what doctor, nurse, or psychologist would ever want to be destructive to his patient? That is not compatible with good medicine or psychology. But it is the net result of superstition. So, in that sense, it is the exact opposite of spiritual healing.

*Leichtman:* You seem to be suggesting that the essential ingredient of healing is the quality of the healer's consciousness—his or her reverence for life.

*Schweitzer:* Yes.

*Leichtman:* Which is not really something you would learn, let's say, in a weekend course on "How to Become a Happy Healer."

*Schweitzer:* You can't obtain a reverence for life from someone else. You have to cultivate it within yourself. That means going through the careful, step-by-step training a mystic would go through. That starts with the long process of getting to know yourself, as the Greeks taught it. I'm not talking about getting to know your hang-ups, your feelings, and your wishes, although you will have to learn to control them. I'm talking about getting to know your spirit, your wisdom, your love, and your potential. I'm talking about getting to know the healing force within you—and the ultimate truth about who you are.

As you do this, you'll develop some of the gifts that will let you operate more fully at inner levels—gifts like clairvoyance and psychic ability. But you must not confuse these gifts of the inner life with the inner life itself. People who stop searching for the ultimate truth about themselves after they develop a bit of psychic ability or clairvoyance are letting themselves get stuck on the wrong level. Being clairvoyant or psychic is no guarantee of an ability to heal. That comes by being able to touch the healing force within you.

*Leichtman:* What would you recommend to someone interested in contacting this healing force? Will reading books help, or meditating, or what?

*Schweitzer:* Reading the right books could be useful, yes. There's a lot of good information about the nature of the healing force, for example, in the little book the two of you wrote, *The Way To Health*. Meditation can be helpful, too. But just reading books and meditating is not the whole story.

*Leichtman:* What else should be done?

*Schweitzer:* Primarily, practicing what we've been discussing throughout this entire interview. That is, reaching inward and knowing that there are divine elements within you, within the patient, and within the universe that can help you do your work as a doctor, a nurse, or a psychologist. You are not alone in wanting to help this person; you are not alone in caring about his or her well-being. And so, you focus your own deep concern for the well-being of your patient, and work with the confidence that there are other, greater forces of caring and healing being focused through your individual concern and efforts.

Now, that may not seem as spectacular as some of the techniques taught in the weekend seminars, but it's the real key to spiritual healing. The capacity to love and nurture the health of your patients is the single most important feature of all healing.

*Japikse:* That sounds like something that would take a whole lifetime to cultivate.

*Schweitzer:* Well, it does grow and mature slowly, step by step. There's no such thing as instant enlightenment.

*Leichtman:* Yes, and I think that's something your own life demonstrated very nicely. Your maturity and understanding seemed to evolve, become richer, and acquire more meaning as you went from experience to experience. And that greater maturity was reflected in your writings.

*Schweitzer:* That's the way life is. If you are a person who expects to attain instant enlightenment, you are probably also a person who will stop after making very little progress, and just stay there, believing that you've accomplished what you set out to do. You've gained your instant's worth, and so you stop. But if I was going to name the worst sin I could think of, that would be it.

*Leichtman:* What would be it?

*Schweitzer:* To stop growing. To stop enriching your life and your thinking.

*Leichtman:* Well, you certainly were not guilty of that sin. I would hope some of our readers will be inspired to pick up your life story and study it, because it's an excellent example of what we're talking about here. You would involve yourself in extremely intense work, either in Africa or in your concert and lecture tours of Europe, but then there were also periods in your life when you had a little more time to yourself. It's obvious to me that it was during the periods of intense involvement that you really grew; the quiet times of reading and meditation served more to consolidate the meaning of recent activities and to prepare you for new growth.

*Schweitzer:* I think that's basically true. From the perspective of the inner life, all experiences of daily living are opportunities to grow, to serve, to love. They all contribute to what you do. Meditating is important, but it doesn't do the whole job. One has to act in the world.

*Leichtman:* Is this what you mean, then, by the idea of Christian service to our fellow man—that there is something enriching about the work of service in addition to knowing you are helping someone else?

*Schweitzer:* Absolutely. When you are engaged in proper works of service, you always receive more than you give. That's the marvelous aspect of love: you are always enriched by expressing it, never impoverished. You get back more than you give. Both the giver and the one who receives the gift therefore benefit.

*Leichtman:* To my mind, this is one of the most central ingredients of the Christian religion, when properly understood—the need to work in service, to help one another. That concept isn't as strong in other major religions, is it? Did you find, for example, many Hindu or Moslem missionaries or hospitals?

*Schweitzer:* I wasn't aware of any; there may not have been any in all Africa. But I really don't know.

*Leichtman:* The Christian religion has sponsored many hospitals and orphanages throughout the centuries, but I don't recall that being a major concern in other religions, except Judaism.

*Schweitzer:* Judaism, of course, is the foundation on which Christianity was built. No, I doubt that there were any Moslem or Hindu hospitals.

*Leichtman:* What do you think of the holistic

health movement in medicine today?

*Schweitzer:* It's a marvelous idea, an idea whose time has come. There's some nonsense associated with it, of course, but that's always the case when any good idea gets started.

*Leichtman:* Do you have any specific warning or advice as to what to look for?

*Schweitzer:* Results. *[Laughter.]*

*Leichtman:* Can you be more specific?

*Schweitzer:* If an unorthodox treatment works, then go ahead and use it. If it doesn't, then try something else that does.

*Leichtman:* That would seem to be an effective way of measuring almost anything.

*Schweitzer:* If it were used, it would quickly eliminate a lot of the silly ideas that have been coming up. By and large, however, the people who are behind the current movement are sensible enough to do this.

*Leichtman:* Yes, they are. Well, to continue this line of thought, from your current perspective, what would you like to see people in medicine do next?

*Schweitzer:* Become more aware, in their training and their practice, of how much the quality of their concern for the patient does actually contribute to the healing process. Many health professionals, unfortunately, never really love their patients enough. And when that happens, it cuts the heart out of our profession.

The extreme, of course, is the doctor who gets all wrapped up in his investments and his luxuries, and his office becomes a money mill. That kind of doctor should not be in practice—or, at least, he should re-evaluate the meaning of his practice. But that's probably a good idea for all health professionals, not just the ones at the ridiculous extreme. We should all be in the habit of reevaluating the meaning of our practice, on a regular basis. Because that's the only way we can increase the usefulness of what we do. And, as much as possible, we should reevaluate how we can be more caring, more loving.

*Leichtman:* Yes. What do you think about the movement to teach patients the value of controlling their own attitudes toward health, and assuming responsibility for it?

*Schweitzer:* That's an idea of major importance to medicine. It certainly deserves attention—patients need to become aware of the healing force within them, even more so than doctors. And not just become aware of it, but learn to cooperate with it.

*Leichtman:* Do you have any other advice for the medical profession?

*Schweitzer:* Medicine should be doing ten times more good for people than it is now. For one thing, I would like to see more emphasis put on the new trend to approach healing in terms of a medicine of wellness and a psychology of wellness. The emphasis should be on promoting healthiness, not on sickness.

*Leichtman:* Yes.

*Schweitzer:* And training patients to be healthy.

*Leichtman:* That expands the concept of healing, so that you don't have to be sick in order to get better.

*Schweitzer:* I'm glad you said that.

*Leichtman:* Well, I wasn't the first.

*Schweitzer:* But in the context of our conversation, it was very apt.

*Leichtman:* It's very obvious to me, from the writings you left behind and the way you conducted your life, that healing meant far more to you than simply caring for sick or diseased people. It involved an improvement or uplifting of consciousness, not just in individuals, but potentially in society, religion, government, and the world as a whole. What should be done to further this work of healing society?

*Schweitzer:* More people have to follow the injunction given us by Jesus, to find the kingdom of heaven within. We must start dealing with reality, both at inner and outer levels. And that means being active at both levels. The inner life must be expressed through active service in the outer world, and everything we do in the outer world should be guided and inspired by our inner life.

I suppose the real key to healing society is the idea behind the title you chose for this series of interviews, *From Heaven to Earth*. As we discover the hidden life of God within ourselves and within society, and bring it into expression in our lives collectively, we heal society. As we bring heaven to earth, and build new awareness of the kingdom of heaven among the peoples of the earth, we heal society.

Ideally, the churches should take the lead in this endeavor, but I am realistic. They probably won't. They are sometimes so busy *following* those who have come and gone that they have little time left to *lead* those who are here. So, the movement to help people discover the kingdom of heaven within them is probably better off separated from the organized church, at the moment.

The early Christians taught each other how to discover the hidden life of God within, but that aspect of the teaching has largely dropped out of the church. It's a very bad thing that it was dropped; that kind of teaching ought to be part of the work of the church. It was stopped for political reasons, I believe.

*Leichtman:* Let me go back to music again, which was obviously one of your great loves in life. You gave concert tours, wrote books, and even made recordings. I have the impression that the music was more interesting to you, and certainly more fun, than your missionary work.

*Schweitzer:* Yes. Of course, in doing all that, I was earning money to help support the clinic. And, it was self-healing, too.

*Leichtman:* If you had had your druthers, what would have been the most enjoyable way to spend your career?

*Schweitzer:* Essentially, I *did* have my druthers. I did what I really wanted to do.

*Japikse:* Was that because being a missionary "felt good," or because you had a real dedication to that work?

*Schweitzer:* Well, of course, it was because I had a real dedication—very much so. When the opportunity came, I thought, "Ah-ha, that's what I want to do." And even when I was depressed by the nature of my work, that work was still what I wanted to do. I had thought it through; it was a strong conviction with me.

*Japikse:* Well, we have both observed people who make a big show of performing "service" to mankind, but the service they choose is really not a service at all, it's just a thinly-disguised gratification of their own emotional desires.

*Leichtman:* Yes, they are camouflaging their selfishness as service. But it is quite clear that you were performing genuine service. You were not just doing what you really enjoyed. You undoubtedly enjoyed what you did, just as we enjoy what we do, but your purpose in doing it was not just to satisfy your emotions or ego.

*Schweitzer:* That's true. I did what I wanted to do, but the "want" was based on a conviction about the value of service, not emotional gratification. I thought it was the most useful way to live my life.

It was determined by the values I held—the value of being able to do some good, the value of being a proper Christian.

*Leichtman:* Would those values be best described as feelings, thoughts, or a dedication?

*Schweitzer:* Values involve all three—they involve your whole being. They originate in spirit, but they aren't worth much unless your personality and your feelings embrace them, too. When a man gets in the proper perspective with God, the choices of what he is going to do with his life become obvious. And they are the right choices.

*Leichtman:* Of the three most significant areas of your life, your music, your philosophy, and your medical practice, which was the most difficult?

*Schweitzer:* The medicine, of course, but I don't want to sound like I was a martyr. Much of the time, the hardship was a beautiful experience, and a satisfying and fulfilling experience, in its way. I was able to overcome my fatigue and limitations and keep on working.

I never considered myself a martyr, because I always had great help from the spirit. The work of service is never easy—or it wouldn't be true service. This is part of service; you have to cast yourself in a role where the personality alone cannot do the work required. To achieve your goals, you have to call forth the life of the spirit. And as you do, you bring more of heaven to earth.

Once you realize this about service, it does become a joyous experience—even the hardships. As Jesus said, "My yoke is easy, my burden is light." That is a very profound statement.

*Leichtman:* Some people might say that the combination of music, philosophy, and medicine was rather odd. Was there a unifying theme which connected them for you, or were they simply three distinct activities?

*Schweitzer:* There was a common denominator, but I'm not sure I can easily explain what it was. Let me put it this way. Each of these was an expression of the best within me—and the best expression I could make.

*Japikse:* When you say, "an expression of the best within you," what exactly do you mean? Some people would just assume it was the best way you could show yourself off.

*Schweitzer:* No, I wasn't trying to show myself off. I accepted duty as a value, and I felt I had a duty to express the talent I had in those three areas. I owed myself the expression of those three facets of my personality.

*Leichtman:* You owed it to your personality or to your spirit?

*Schweitzer:* To my spirit, of course.

*Leichtman:* In other words, this self-expression was a way of honoring your spiritual duty.

*Schweitzer:* Yes. And so, the common denominator of these three expressions would be *me*. Not me the personality, but me the spirit. They all became the same thing to me, because each was an opportunity to contribute something of my spirit to life.

Let me add this, too. By expressing myself in these three ways, I honored God. I looked for God's love, and I found His beauty and wisdom, too. I found God's music, God's ethics, and God's healing power. That's why I say these three expressions all became the same expression to me.

And this is true for many people, I think. They seek God and suddenly have a major breakthrough, leading to a new appreciation of every aspect of their life.

*Japikse:* If I might play the devil's advocate a moment, a little while ago you said that the marvelous thing about service is that the one who serves always receives back more than he gives. And we've just been talking about self-expression. I can easily imagine some readers might misconstrue these statements as advocating selfishness.

*Schweitzer:* Well, a certain measure of what I might call ''enlightened selfishness'' is necessary in order to live life in the physical plane. I'm not talking about ordinary selfishness, however.

*Japikse:* Is there perhaps a less confusing way to describe this ''enlightened selfishness''?

*Schweitzer:* Enlightened selfishness can be thought of in terms of living your life in a responsible way—making sure that you support yourself, educate yourself, and do what you can to enrich human life. It would include what we've been talking about today—

reaching inward for the truth.

The ordinary variety of selfishness, however, tends to be just the opposite. It rejects responsibility for one's own life, and demands indulgence and pampering from others. They can both be called "selfish," because they are "of the self," but the difference is great. The person who rejects responsibility is very sick of mind.

*Japikse:* Would it perhaps be better to label this "enlightened selfishness" as a love of selfhood—or a love of the God within?

*Schweitzer:* In general, yes, but it is also useful for people to take the apparent contradiction of the phrase "enlightened selfishness" and toy with it in their minds until they understand *how* it means "the love of the God within." Keep in mind, in this context, that the word "ego" generally is used in a negative sense, but the word means, very simply, "I am." Now, some people would give the phrase "I am" a negative connotation, but I don't at all.

Before you can serve, or love, or heal, you have to be able to express "I am." You must be able to be selfish in an enlightened manner. The goal of humanity, after all, is not to eliminate selfishness, but to enlighten it. And it is important for individuals to have the desire to learn as much as they can in a lifetime, to experience as much as they can in a lifetime, and to reach inward and find God and then turn outward and honor Him through self-expression.

It's important for people to wake up, suddenly one morning, and discover that they have a lovely, gorgeous continent within them, that's just begging to be explored. That's an awakening from ordinary selfishness into enlightened selfishness.

*Japikse:* What would you say is the proper motivation for service?

*Schweitzer:* The need to be useful. That sounds a little egotistical, but it is necessary to live life being needed and being useful.

*Japikse:* No, I don't think that sounds egotistical, because it implies that you have something worthwhile to offer, and you are giving it freely. You are not just going around spreading your good intentions.

*Schweitzer:* The line from the Bible that I quoted before, "By their acts ye shall know them," applies again here. The person who is serving with the wrong motivation will be exposed by the quality of his service. But the true Christian will be motivated by his concern for his fellow man.

*Japikse:* Yes. Well, having spent your life in service, what advice would you give to others who would serve, but are not sure where to start?

*Leichtman:* Should they all rush off to Africa to do missionary work?

*Schweitzer:* Not at all. There are plenty of opportunities to serve in the context of your own environment and circumstances. The place to start, of course, is wherever there is a need that can be met by a talent or gift you can contribute. So, start by looking for legitimate needs in your own family and work, and then evaluate your capacities—the capacities of your spirit, too—to meet those needs.

If you don't have the talents or gifts to meet a specific need, but feel especially drawn to serving in that area, then take the time to carefully train yourself so you can.

*Japikse:* Yes, I believe that's what you did—you did not actually start studying medicine until after you had decided to serve as a doctor. Are there glamours that people, especially Christians, develop about the value of service which end up interfering with the true purposes of service?

*Schweitzer:* I'm sorry, I'm not sure I understand how you are using the word "glamour."

*Japikse:* It's not a common usage of it. I'm referring to illusions or fascinations that people, especially Christians, might develop about service.

*Schweitzer:* I suppose you're referring to the fact that many people view service as a way of chalking up "brownie points" or "credit" in heaven. In fact, many of them believe that the more unpleasant or uncomfortable they are while serving, the more "brownie points" they'll get. But it doesn't work that way—that is an illusion. In terms of service, doing the right thing for the wrong reasons is simply wrong. It doesn't qualify as service.

*Japikse:* In your writings, you described a certain fatigue in civilization. We talked about pessimism and depression earlier, but this is a little different, as though you had the impression that this fatigue was stressing civilization. Is this fatigue still present, and if so, how does it affect modern civilization?

*Schweitzer:* Yes, the fatigue is still present. It is like a cancer in society. It can be seen among people who are not willing to take responsibility for their acts and thoughts, and in the governments which cater to them. It can also be seen in governments that refuse to let the people take this responsibility and tell them, "Oh, no, you aren't supposed to think for yourself.

We'll think for you."

*Japikse:* What is required to revitalize society and civilization?

*Schweitzer:* For people to take responsibility for their own lives and actions.

*Japikse:* Does that have its correspondence in terms of civilization and large groups of people, too?

*Schweitzer:* The American civilization would be a good example of that, yes. It is designed to let people take responsibility for themselves, but many Americans have refused to take it. They have not made the choice—and you *do* have to make a choice.

*Leichtman:* Very good. Before we finish, I want to ask you what activities occupy your time now. How do you keep yourself busy?

*Schweitzer:* I continue to be concerned with the reverence for life, both here and in the physical world. I'm active with a large group of people who are involved in service to the world, each on his own plane; I try to show them what it means to be helpful in the world, what it means to love God and His creation, and what it means to find God—and that it is really the most utterly simple and rational and natural event of life. Finding God should be even more simple and natural than breathing, because we are designed to be loving and caring individuals. We are designed to be helpful.

But the impulse to help can be polluted by our desire for attention and self-aggrandizement; we can get fuzzy in our understanding of what is helpful and what is not. So I am helping people who want to serve to straighten out their understanding of the reverence for life and how to apply it. I am helping these people purify some of their feelings and intentions.

I am also active in some areas of medicine, by assisting those who are dedicated to being a healing influence on their patients. I'm even active in some of the research being done into the use of sound in healing. I don't mean to imply that I'm working with a scientist who's making a gadget that will be released soon and heal millions of people. Sometimes the sound that heals is your own reassuring voice, saying, "There, there. I understand what you're going through, and I know it's difficult, but we can help you manage this with reasonable comfort." It's not the sound of someone singing or screaming.

*Japikse:* Gee, I thought you were in heaven chanting the sacred names of God all day long. *[Laughter.]*

*Schweitzer:* No. The only way we sound the name of God is by doing His will and serving His creation. That really is the only dance there is, to use a well-worn phrase. It's the only activity that counts. On the inner side of life, of course, a chant is a form of dance. "Chanting"—and I'm not talking about physically chanting—makes matter vibrate in a certain pattern so that it begins to dance up and down, in a sense, and rearrange itself in new patterns. That's why I used the term "dance."

Isn't that fascinating?

*Japikse:* Oh, yes.

*Schweitzer:* Well, I haven't said anything really useful.

*Leichtman:* No, but it makes a nice chant.

*[Laughter.]*

*Japikse:* When you say you are active helping people, what do you mean? I know what you mean, but some of our readers may not. How can you, as a spook, help someone in physical form?

*Schweitzer:* Well, I didn't mean to imply that everyone I help is physical.

*Japikse:* Sure.

*Schweitzer:* When I was in the physical, there was a large group of spirits I worked with, and I continue to work as part of this group. We help one another focus certain qualities of energy, and then send them on to the physical world. In fact, this is the work of many groups "up here." We summon aspects of God's wisdom or love and then project them to certain areas of the world, or groups, or specific people. There has always been, and still is, an urgent need for compassion, caring, tenderness, and gentleness in the world. We try to help meet that need.

Sometimes, we bring people into our little group and they learn from us by watching us, and by absorbing our frequency of energy. Some of these are people who are incarnate. They visit us during the hours of their sleep, travel with us on our rounds, and pick up some of our qualities of thought and consciousness, I guess by osmosis. At other times, we try to feed and sustain the goodwill and good intentions of individuals who have a capacity for reverence for life. We don't do their work for them, but we do help energize their good ideas and intentions and help nourish their love for the world and for their fellow man.

*Leichtman:* Can you tell us more about this group you work with?

*Schweitzer:* What would you like to know?

*Japikse:* Is it organized in any way, or just—

*Schweitzer:* In our state, organization is unnecessary. We all see the common goal clearly.

*Japikse:* Isn't there structure to the work?

*Schweitzer:* Oh, there is structure to the work, but we work in a state of harmony that would be impossible on the physical plane at the present time, except among rare individuals. We are very much in tune with each other, and we don't have to waste a lot of time discussing what we are going to do, because we each know what it is we have to do.

*Leichtman:* No committee meetings?

*Schweitzer:* We don't need them.

*Leichtman:* No political bickerings to see who runs the show? *[Laughter.]*

*Schweitzer:* There would be no place for that.

*Japikse:* Does everyone on your side of the veil work together in such perfect harmony?

*Schweitzer:* Oh, I was talking about the specific group I belong to.

If I may, I'd like to close with this thought. In physical life, I was a healer of sick bodies and minds. I did other things, but that was one of the major roles I played. And what I did in my work in Africa I now do on a larger scale. It's the same type of work, but now I'm working more to be a healing influence on certain segments of society and mass consciousness. I am actually dealing with almost the same forces and energies I dealt with in the physical—it's the same frame of mind. I'm still very much aware of the nobility and greatness that God has created within every person, and I'm still very much aware that you nurture this seed of greatness with love. So, in a very real sense, I'm continuing the same work I did in the physical.

I hope that more people will join me, too—not in

my work, but in the realization of what it means to nurture the seed of life with love. I hope they will join me in finding their own unique connection with God within themselves, in finding that His love is also their love, and in finding that they, in union with God, can become healers in their own lives and their own circumstances.

That's the message I had the honor to deliver to the world. I talked about it a bit, I wrote about it a bit, but I think it's the service I performed that really delivered the message. That's always the case: it's what anyone is actually able to achieve that becomes the message of his or her life.

What I did, everyone can do. And I hope one day everyone is able to do as well as I did, or better. That's what we are designed to do, after all—we are designed to be vehicles of God's wisdom and love. That was my message as Albert Schweitzer—and it still is.

It hasn't changed a bit.

# GLOSSARY

*ASPIRANT:* One who actively seeks to be more attuned to the inner life of spirit, and better able to express it in his or her daily circumstances.

*CLAIRVOYANCE:* The capacity to see or know beyond the limits of the physical senses. There are many degrees of clairvoyance, allowing the clairvoyant to comprehend forces, beings, and objects of the inner worlds normally invisible to the average person.

*DIMENSION:* A measurement of size, space, movement, or consciousness. There can be dimensions of thought and feeling as well as physical dimensions.

*DREAM IMAGE:* The kind of image or symbol which would normally be perceived by the average person in a dream state, while asleep. These images, however, can be perceived by psychics and clairvoyants in other states of consciousness as well. Dream images can be personal, generated by the wishes, desires, emotions, or memories of one individual; or collective, generated by the wishes, desires, emotions, or memories of mass consciousness.

*ENLIGHTENMENT:* Focused in the light of the inner life of spirit. An enlightened mind is one that is capable of directly contacting this inner life and using its light to perceive, comprehend, and apply the spirit's wisdom. An enlightened personality is one that is governed and directed by an enlightened mind, in tune with the wisdom and love of the spirit.

*ESOTERIC:* An adjective which refers to knowledge of the inner worlds and inner life. In this book, it is used to refer to the knowledge of spirit—and to the body of teachings known as the Ancient Wisdom.

*EVIL:* Anything which retards the evolution of human consciousness. Contrary to public opinion, evil is not measured by our likes and dislikes. Unpleasant experiences may help us evolve, and would therefore not be evil. By contrast, the indulgence of one person by another may be pleasant—but quite harmful.

*FAITH:* The attitude which attunes the personality to the wisdom, love, and power of the inner life of spirit. Enlightened faith motivates us to aspire to higher expressions of our humanity and intelligence, to serve God, and to fulfill our destiny. It creates a channel for prayer, healing, and creativity. In no way, however, should faith be misconstrued to signify "blind belief," in God or in anything else. Faith is based on heartfelt knowing, not belief.

*GLAMOUR:* Before the word acquired its modern popular meaning, it meant "an enchantment" or "magic spell." In esoteric writings, the word still preserves this basic meaning, and is used in a technical sense to refer to the illusions and distortions of reality generated by the emotions, either of an individual or of mass consciousness. Fears and worries, for example, would be negative glamours, because they cast a spell on the thinking apparatus of the person who is afraid or worried, deluding him. Strong wishes and fantasies would also be glamours, although more pleasant by nature. Dispelling glamour is one of the great challenges the spiritual aspirant must face—and one of the most difficult.

*GURU:* A Hindu term for "teacher."

*HEAVEN:* The state of consciousness of the spirit. Heaven is not a place populated by those who have died; it is accessible to incarnate and discarnate humans alike. It is a state of mind. In heaven are located the archetypal patterns of all creation, as well as the ideal qualities of human expression. Heaven, therefore, is the source of all expressions of genius and saintliness.

*HELL:* A very low state of consciousness, devoid of contact with the spirit. Like heaven, hell is not a place populated by those who have died; its population includes incarnate and discarnate humans alike. It is a state of mind, induced by strong and negative emotions such as despair, greed, possessiveness, bitterness, malice, lust, and excessive selfishness. The principal characteristic of hell is its sense of emptiness, nothingness, and lack of meaning. It is symbolically referred to as "the outer darkness."

*HOLISTIC HEALTH:* A movement in medicine which aims to treat the health of the whole person—spiritual, mental, and emotional, as well as physical. It sees these different states of health as interrelated; therefore, as the health of any one level improves, it contributes to the health of the other levels, too.

*INNER LIFE:* The unconscious dimensions of our

individuality and activity as a human being. The term covers a very broad gamut, ranging from our activities while asleep and dreaming on the one hand to the creative and healing work of the spirit on the other.

*LAYING ON OF HANDS:* A technique of spiritual healing, in which the healing force of spirit is focused, in part, through the hands, in addition to the heart and the mind of the healer.

*LIGHT:* Esoterically, there are many octaves of light, of which visible light is the densest. In its higher octaves, light is consciousness itself.

*MAGIC:* In its original sense, the acts of a Magus or wise person with conscious awareness of the inner life of spirit. Pure magic, therefore, is the focusing of creative energies for the transformation of forms. It brings heaven to earth and enriches the earth. Ordinary forms of ''magic'' are distortions of this original meaning.

*MASS CONSCIOUSNESS:* Literally, the mind and emotions of the human race as a single whole. To some degree, the thinking and feeling of every human being contributes to mass consciousness and—to a much larger degree—is powerfully influenced and conditioned by mass consciousness.

*MASTER:* A term used by esoteric students to refer to an individual who has reached complete competence and perfection as a human. The epitome of genius.

*MEDITATION:* An act of mental rapport in which the ideals, purposes, and intents of the inner life are discerned, interpreted, and applied by the personality. To be meaningful, meditation must be a very active state in which creative ideas, new realizations, and inspirations are pursued with vigor. The current belief that meditation is a passive state of emptying the mind, by concentrating on a mantra or by just ''sitting,'' is the antithesis of true meditation.

*MEDIUM:* A person who practices mediumship, the phenomenon of a nonphysical intelligence, usually a discarnate human, assuming some degree of control of a physical body in order to communicate something meaningful and useful.

*MIND:* The portion of the human personality that has the capacity to think. The mind is an organized field of energy which exists in invisible dimensions. It is *not* the physical brain, although it does operate through the brain during physical life.

*MYSTICISM:* The process of loving, revering, and *finding* God and His entire creation.

*PERSONALITY:* The part of the human being that is used for manifestation in the earth plane. It is composed of a mind, a set of emotions, and a physical body, each containing conscious and subconscious functions. It is the child of the inner life and its experiences on earth.

*PSYCHIC:* A person who is able to perceive events and information without the use of the physical senses. The word is also used to refer to any event associated with the phenomena of parapsychology.

*SELF:* A psychological term used to describe the center of the totality of the unconscious and conscious aspects of the human being. The self acts to unite and integrate the diverse elements of the individual.

*SPIRIT:* In this book, a word used primarily to describe the highest immortal, divine essence within the human being. Both incarnate and discarnate humans alike possess this spirit within them. In popular usage, however, the word is used to refer to the portion of the human being which survives death. In this sense, a spirit would be as individualistic as his or her personality was during physical life, retaining both good and bad characteristics. This second usage is also used to some degree in this interview.

*SPIRITUAL HEALING:* The healing of physical, emotional, and mental disorders through invocation of the power of the human spirit. There are many varieties of spiritual healing and many levels of competence among those who claim to heal spiritually. This form of healing differs from the usual varieties of ''faith healing'' in that it taps the light of spirit and uses it as a source of health. ''Faith healing'' taps only the emotional wish to be well.

*SPOOK:* An affectionate term for a discarnate.

*SUBCONSCIOUS:* The part of the personality that is not being consciously used at any given moment. The subconscious is always active and greatly influences our conscious moods, thoughts, acts, and attitudes. It is psychically in tune with other portions of the inner planes—even if we are not consciously psychic at all.

*SYMBOL:* An image, thought, feeling, or event which contains a deeper significance than what is obvious from the outer form. It points to inner dimensions of reality, force, and meaning. To discern these inner dimensions, however, the symbol must be interpreted. The study of symbolism is useful only if it leads to a discovery of the reality that the symbol veils.

*VIBRATION:* The movement of any energy particle, whether physical, astral, or mental in origin. The word is popularly used to refer to emanations of astral energy which are perceived by psychic sensitivity.

*WITCHCRAFT:* A debased form of occultism, in which the goal is to manipulate physical and astral energy for the purposes of the personality. The goal of true occultism, by contrast, is to advance the life of the spirit. Witchcraft, therefore, is the exact opposite of occultism.

# FROM HEAVEN TO EARTH

Both series of 12 interviews are available by subscription for $27 *each* (for foreign delivery, including Canada, $30), or $50 together ($55 for foreign delivery). Each interview is published as a paperback book.

The spirits interviewed in the first series of 12 are Edgar Cayce, William Shakespeare, Cheiro, Carl Jung and Sigmund Freud, C.W. Leadbeater, Sir Oliver Lodge, Thomas Jefferson, Arthur Ford, H.P. Blavatsky, Nikola Tesla, Eileen Garrett, and Stewart White. All 12 books are now in print.

The spirits interviewed in the second series of 12 are Albert Schweitzer, Rembrandt, Sir Winston Churchill, Paramahansa Yogananda, Mark Twain, Albert Einstein, Benjamin Franklin, Andrew Carnegie, Richard Wagner, Luther Burbank, and Abraham Lincoln. The final book will be an interview with a number of spirits, titled *The Destiny of America*. All 12 books are now in print.

Orders can be placed by sending a check for the proper amount to Ariel Press, P.O. Box 20580, Columbus, Ohio 43220. Make checks payable to Ariel Press. Foreign checks should be payable in U.S. funds. In Ohio, please add 5½% sales tax. *Be sure to specify which set of books you are purchasing (first or second series).*

Individual copies of the interviews are available at $3.50 plus $1 postage each. If 10 or more copies of *a single title* are ordered at one time, the price is $2.50 a book plus the actual costs of shipping.

# ACTIVE MEDITATION

Meditation is a set of practices which help us bring the life and power of the higher self into expression in the daily activities of the personality. The regular use of meditation enriches consciousness, illumines the mind, increases self-discipline, stimulates creativity, and integrates the personality with the higher self.

Effective meditation has been part of every significant spiritual tradition in human history—because there is no better way of establishing contact between the personality and the higher self. And yet, not all systems of meditation lead to enlightenment. In many systems, the art of meditation has been trivialized. Instead of serving as a method for establishing contact with the higher self, it has become a simple process of relaxing or quieting the mind and body. Many people accept these practices as legitimate aspects of meditation, but they are not.

*Active Meditation: The Western Tradition* sets the record straight. Written by Robert R. Leichtman, M.D. and Carl Japikse, it is a comprehensive examination of the tradition, purpose, potential, and techniques of meditation. More importantly, it is a masterful statement of the emerging Western tradition of personal and spiritual growth. It is a book which challenges, inspires, enlightens, and informs.

The tone set by Dr. Leichtman and Mr. Japikse emphasizes the practical nature of meditation. To them, the subjects of meditation and personal growth are inseparable—the work of meditation should always be connected with the development of a greater capacity to act wisely and creatively in the physical plane.

*Active Meditation: The Western Tradition* is therefore something more than just a precise definition of the art of meditation. It is also a thorough commentary on personal and spiritual growth. In specific, the authors describe:
- What meditation is—and is not.
- How meditation accelerates growth.
- The nature of the higher self.
- How to contact the higher self.
- The work of integration.
- The skills of meditation and how to use them.
- Seven specific techniques of Active Meditation.
- Meditating to help others.
- Group meditations.

Throughout, the constant goal of the authors is to strip away the vagueness and obscurity often associated with meditation and treat their subject with common sense, clarity, detailed explanations, and good humor. *Active Meditation: The Western Tradition* is easy to read and understand—and yet has also been acclaimed as *the* standard reference book on meditation. In many ways, it is the most encyclopedic book ever written on the subject, filled with information vital to everyone who meditates—and everyone interested in personal and spiritual growth.

*Active Meditation: The Western Tradition* is 512 pages, hardbound, and includes a glossary and index. It can be purchased at all leading bookstores or directly from Ariel Press for $24.50 plus $1.50 for postage ($2.50 outside of the U.S.). To order, send a check or money order in U.S. funds to Ariel Press, P.O. Box 20580, Columbus, Ohio 43220.

# THE WORK OF LIGHT

Light is a nonprofit charitable foundation which seeks to stimulate the growth of the mind and the creativity of people throughout the world. One important way it is pursuing this goal is through the publications of Ariel Press—by making quality writings on the mind, intuition, health, and creativity readily available.

Other activities of the work of Light include the Books of Light, a book club, lectures, and research into the use of the mind.

The work of Light is supported by its contributing members. Members of Light receive a series of lessons in personal growth called *Enlightenment*, a newsletter called ''The Work of Light,'' membership in Books of Light, and reduced rates on cassette tapes.

The cost of a contributing membership is $25 per year for an individual, $40 per year for a family. There are also three other levels of contributing membership: the *fellow* ($100 a year), the *benefactor* ($250 a year), and the *angel* ($1,000 a year). Fellows, benefactors, and angels are entitled to a 20 percent discount on all books they buy from Ariel Press.

To become a member of Light, send a check and a letter of application to Light, P.O. Box 20580, Columbus, Ohio 43220. Contributions to Light are fully tax deductible.

Light is also looking for special gifts to its Publications Fund, over and above membership dues, to continue funding the publication of books such as *From Heaven to Earth*, and the other books it issues.